FURTHER *Curriculum Bank* ACTIVITIES

Helena Rothwell

READING

KEY STAGE TWO / SCOTTISH LEVELS C–E

C000040990

GEORGE HUNT

Published by Scholastic Ltd,
Villiers House,
Clarendon Avenue,
Leamington Spa,
Warwickshire CV32 5PR
Text © George Hunt
© 1999 Scholastic Ltd
1234567890 9012345678

Author
George Hunt

Editor
Kate Pearce

Assistant Editor
Roanne Davis

Series designer
Rachel Warner

Designer
Rachael Hammond

Illustrations
Paula Martyr

Cover illustration
Lesley Saddington

Scottish 5–14 links
Margaret Scott and Susan Gow

Acknowledgements
Department for Education and Employment and the
Controller of Her Majesty's Stationery Office for the use of
extracts from the *National Literacy Strategy: Framework for
Teaching* © Crown copyright 1998
A.C. Cooper for photographs of the front cover illustrations
© 1999, A.C. Cooper

British Library Cataloguing-in-Publication Data
A catalogue record for this book is available from
the British Library.

ISBN 0-590-53872-1

The right of George Hunt to be identified as the Author of
this Work has been asserted by him in accordance with
the Copyright, Designs and Patents Act 1988.

All rights reserved. This book is sold subject to the
condition that it shall not, by way of trade or otherwise, be
lent, hired out or otherwise circulated without the
publisher's prior consent in any form of binding or cover
other than that in which it is published and without a
similar condition, including this condition, being imposed
upon the subsequent purchaser.

No part of this publication may be reproduced, stored in a
retrieval system, or transmitted, in any form or by any
means, electronic, mechanical, photocopying, recording or
otherwise, without the prior permission of the publisher.
This book remains copyright, although permission is
granted to copy those pages marked 'photocopiable' for
classroom distribution and use only in the school which
has purchased the book or by the teacher who has
purchased the book and in accordance with the CLA
licensing agreement. Photocopying permission is given
for purchasers only and not for borrowers of books from
any lending service.

Contents

Introduction

In both the National Curriculum and the National Literacy Strategy, great emphasis is placed upon the need for children to read a variety of texts, and to acquire word- and sentence-level skills through reflection on these texts, as well as through direct teaching. Accordingly, this book follows the same procedure as the preceding *Curriculum Bank Reading, Key Stage Two* book in grounding most of the suggested activities within the context of whole stories, reports, procedural texts, poems and various types of environmental print.

Those activities which are not based on exploration of such 'whole texts' are presented as linguistic games and investigations, aimed at whetting children's curiosity about words and larger units of language as objects of interetin their own right. In recent years there has been an increasing recognition of children's seemingly inherent curiosity about the workings of language, and their readiness to play with and extemporize on the language that they hear and see around them. This inquisitiveness and flexibility has a great deal of potential for promoting the development of literacy, and ideas for nurturing these qualities are offered in every chapter.

As with *Curriculum Bank Reading, Key Stage Two*, the main aim is to help the teacher to meet the challenge of teaching a wide range of skills to a wide range of attainment levels, without confining children who are at the beginning stages of learning to read to drills in so called basic skills. The book is based on the general principle that such aspects of reading as critical awareness and personal response are fundamental, and should be encouraged at all stages.

All of the activities are intended to act as blueprints for general procedures which teachers can initially try out using suggested books or photocopiables, and then adapt to other material appropriate for the age range and interests of the children you teach. The majority of the activities are compatible with the structure of the Literacy Hour, and specific suggestions for working within this framework have been made. However, many activities have a more open time frame. They might be initiated within the Literacy Hour, then revisited at more depth in subsequent parts of any appropriate time. It is important to remember that literacy extends beyond the Literacy Hour. Many of the activities start from topics more commonly associated with subject areas other than English. At a time when boundaries between subjects are becoming more impermeable, the idea of language across the curriculum is one that needs to be preserved and revived.

Lesson plans

Detailed lesson plans, under clear headings, are given for each activity and provide material for immediate implementation in the classroom. The structure for each activity is as follows.

Activity title box

The box at the beginning of each activity outlines the following key aspects:

▲ *Learning objective.* The learning objectives break down aspects of the programmes of study for English into manageable teaching and learning chunks. They can easily be referenced to the National Curriculum for England and Wales and the Scottish National Guidelines 5–14 by using the overview grid on pages 7–12.

▲ *Class organization/Likely duration.* The icons †† and ⊕ indicate the suggested group sizes for each activity and the approximate amount of time required to complete it.

Previous skills/knowledge needed

This section gives information when it is necessary for the children to have acquired specific knowledge or skills prior to carrying out the activity.

Key background information

This section outlines the areas of study covered by each activity and gives a general background to the particular topic or theme, outlining the basic skills that will be developed and the way in which the activity will address the children's learning.

Preparation

Advice is given when it is necessary for the teacher to prime the pupils for the activity, to prepare materials or to set up a display or activity ahead of time.

Resources needed

All materials needed to carry out the activity, including photocopiable pages, are listed here.

What to do

Clear step-by-step instructions are provided for carrying out the activity. These include (where appropriate) suitable questions for the teacher to ask the children in order to help instigate discussion and stimulate a high quality of writing.

Suggestion(s) for extension/support

In these sections, ways of providing differentiation are suggested.

Assessment opportunities

Where appropriate, opportunities for ongoing teacher assessment of the children's work during or after the activity are highlighted.

Opportunities for IT

Where relevant IT work would strengthen an activity, appropriate possibilities are outlined.

Display ideas

Where they are relevant and innovative, display ideas are incorporated into the activity plans, perhaps illustrated with examples.

Other aspects of the English PoS covered

Inevitably, as all areas of English are interrelated, activities will cover aspects of the programmes of study in other areas of the English curriculum. These links are highlighted under this heading.

Reference to photocopiable sheets

Photocopiable activity sheets are provided for use with particular activities. Small reproductions of these are included in the appropriate lesson plans, together with notes on their use and (where appropriate) suggested answers to questions.

Overview Grid

This grid helps you to track the coverage of the Reading part of the Programme of Study for English at Key Stage Two, or the Scottish National Guidelines for English Language 5–14 at Levels C–E, offered by the activities in this book. For each activity, the relevant statements from the National Curriculum for England and Wales and the Scottish 5–14 Guidelines are indicated (the latter references are given in italics).

Most of the activities in this book are linked to the *Curriculum Bank* for Reading at Key Stage Two/Scottish Levels C–E. These links are indicated by footnotes below the relevant activities. The grid also shows how the activities relate to the Key Objectives set out in the Literacy Framework. So 3.2 T1 indicates Year 3 Term 2 Text Level 1.

FICTION

ACTIVITY TITLE	LEARNING OBJECTIVE	POS/AO	NLS	CONTENT	PAGE
First sentences	To enable children to anticipate the general content of a fictional text by reflecting on its opening sentence. To enhance critical awareness of the devices used by authors to draw readers into the text.	1a; 2b; 3 *Reflect on the writer's ideas and craft, level C*	3.2 T1; 5.1 T1	Children reflect on and make predictions from first sentences.	13
Rotary story, page 27; Mixing the ingredients, page 38					
Comparing versions of classic stories	To familiarize children with significant stories from a range of cultures. To explore a variety of textual devices by which authors have presented their own versions of these stories throughout history. To encourage children to reflect on their responses to these devices, and on their own literary preferences.	1a, c, d; 2b; 3 *Reading for enjoyment, level C*	3.2 T1–2; 3.3 T9; 4.2 T8–9; 4.3 T2; 5.1 T12; 5.2 T1–2; 5.3 T6; 6.2 T9	Children compare different editions of classic stories.	15
Using short stories for group reading discussions	To identify story themes. To discuss characters, settings and plots critically. To refer to and evaluate significant devices within the text. To compare and contrast authors and genres. To compare personal responses with those of other readers.	1a, c, d; 2b; 3 *Awareness of genre, level C*	All text level fiction comprehension objectives	Children are given guidelines for the group discussion of a range of short stories.	17
Themes in fiction, page 36					
Deriving word meanings from context	To infer the meaning of unknown words from context and to generate a range of possible meanings. To use dictionaries to learn or check the definitions of words. To write their own definitions of words.	1a; 2b, c; 3 *Reading for information, level C*	3.1 W17–22, S1	Children make and check hypotheses about meanings of unfamiliar words in a story.	19
Vocabulary choices in fiction	To familiarize readers with the vocabulary typical of fictional genres, and with the effects of departing from typical patterns.	1a; 2b, c; 3 *Awareness of genre, level C*	3.1 S1; 3.2 T1-3, T9–10	Children generate words to fill lexical gaps in traditional story structure.	21
Reconstructing a familiar text, page 19					
Opening paragraphs	To identify the genre of a story by attending to significant details in the text. To explore the expectations that are set up in opening paragraphs. To focus attention on how paragraphs are structured.	1a, c, d; 2b; 3 *Awareness of genre, level D*	5.1 T1, 15	Children predict story content from opening paragraph.	23
What happens next?, page 23; Rotary story, page 27; Mixing the ingredients, page 38					

ACTIVITY TITLE	LEARNING OBJECTIVE	POS/AO	NLS	CONTENT	PAGE
Prediction and sentence structure	To become aware of grammatical devices which create expectations in the reader.	1a, c; 2b; 3 *Reflect on writer's ideas and craft, level D*	3.1 S1; 3.3 T2; 4.2 S3; 6.1 S5	Children complete sentence starters.	25
Tracking cohesive links	To help readers understand how sentences and paragraphs in a narrative are structured and linked together.	1a, c; 2b; 3 *As above*	3.3 S2, 5–6; 4.2 S4; 6.1 S4	Children make diagram links between sentences.	27
Sequencing unfamiliar text, page 24					
Missing pieces	To investigate the styles and voices of traditional story language. To identify typical story themes. To explore narrative order. To develop an active attitude towards reading. To understand aspects of narrative structure.	1a, c, d; 2b; 3 *Awareness of genre, level D*	3.2 T2; 4.1 T2	Children supply missing chunks from two traditional stories.	29
The missing piece, page 26					
Predicting from story items	To encourage children to generate hypotheses about the likely course of a story by reflecting on previous experience of reading narrative.	1a, c, d; 2b; 3 *Reflect on writer's ideas and craft, level D*	3.2 T6, 7, 9; 4.1 T4	Children predict plot of a story given in key items in the story.	31
What happens next?, page 23					
Fostering uncertainty – inferences	To encourage readers to use inference and deduction in interpreting narrative text, and to compare, discuss and evaluate the different interpretations that they arrive at.	1a, c, d; 2b; 3 *Reflect on writer's ideas and craft, level E*	3.3 T2; 4.2 T2	Children suggest reasons for actions taken by characters.	32
Debating ethical judgements	To encourage readers to become more actively and empathetically involved in stories by encouraging them to evaluate the behaviour of characters.	1a, c, d; 2b; 3 *As above*	4.3 T1, 8; 3.3 T5; 3.2 T2, 3; 5.1 T3	Discussion of the morality of action taken by a story character.	34
Who's to blame?, page 30; Tales with a moral, page 31					
Blurb analysis	To familiarize children with the distinctive types of language found on book covers, and to enable them to analyse this language critically.	1a, b, c, d; 2b; 3 *Reflect on writer's ideas and craft, level D*	6.1 T12; 5.3 T13	Analysis of the language of a make-believe book jacket.	35
Time perspectives	To become aware of some of the ways in which authors handle the passing of time in fiction.	1a, c, d; 2b; 3 *As above*	4.1 T3; 6.2 T1	Diagrammatic representation of how events elapse in a story.	37
Constructing a timeline, page 61					
Predicting from settings	To understand how settings might influence events, atmosphere and characters' behaviour in stories. To understand how writers might play on readers' expectations in relation to settings in order to arouse curiosity.	1a, c, d; 2b; 3 *As above*	3.1 T1; 4.2 T1–4; 5.1 T1; 6.1 T1	Discussion and prediction of story context from setting.	39
Rotary story, page 27; Story map, page 32					

ACTIVITY TITLE	LEARNING OBJECTIVE	POS/AO	NLS	CONTENT	PAGE
Character origins	To familiarize children with the literary or historical origins of characters whose names have entered popular culture. To motivate readers to use information sources in order to extend their knowledge of the origins of popular references.	1a, c, d; 2b; 3 *Reading for information, level D*	5.1 T12; 6.2 T9	Discussion and research about familiar names derived from fiction.	40
Visualising characters, page 33					
Common plights	To familiarize children with some common underlying patterns in story structure: predicament, development and resolution.	1a, c, d; 2b; 3 *Awareness of genre, level C*	3.2 T2; 4.2 T8; 4.3 T2, 8; 6.2 T7	Children predict content of a story from the given outline.	42
Themes in fiction, page 36					
A literature timeline	To raise children's awareness of the historical placing of stories and authors, and to encourage them to read fiction from a wider range of historical authors.	1a, b, c, d; 2b; 3 *Reading for enjoyment, level D*	4.3 T10; 5.1 T12; 5. 3 T6; 6.2 T9; 6.3 T6	Children plot books they have read onto a chart according to their date of publication.	43
A literature map	To familiarize children with literature from a wide range of cultures and to encourage them to read more widely.	1a, b, c, d; 2b; 3 *As above*	4.3 T10; 5.1 T12; 5.3 T6; 6.2 T9; 6.3 T6	Children plot books they have read onto a map showing their setting or origin.	45
Themes in fiction, page 36; Reading resources survey, page 43					
Genres within non-fiction	To appreciate that within non-fiction, authors use different language patterns in order to convey different types of information. To identify distinctive features of these genres, including tense. To scan text samples for technical terms and investigate key vocabulary, using dictionaries to check hypotheses based on context and word structure.	1a, b, c; 2b; 3 *Awareness of genre, level D*	5.2 T16; 3.1 T20; 3.1 W13–15; 3.2 W 17–22; 3.3 W12; 4.2 T17, 20; 5.2 W7, T15; 6.1 T13; 6.3 T15–16, S1	Children analyse non-fiction texts, distinguishing between recount and explanatory genres.	46
Formality and authority	To enable children to identify formal and informal aspects of the language of report writing. To compare formal and informal reports, discussing and assessing their reliability. To talk about the sources of information used by writers of purported non-fiction. To develop critical awareness of the author's perception of readership.	1a, b, c; 2b; 3 *Reflect on writer's ideas and craft, level D*	3.1 T20; 4.1 T18, 16; 5.1 T21; 5.3 T14; 6.1 T12; 6.3 T15–17, 19	Comparison of formally and informally written texts, noting features and assessing authenticity.	48
A read aloud-programme, page 50					
Bias in information texts	To enable children to assess the viewpoints from which 'factual' texts are written.	1a, b, c; 2b; 3 *As above*	4.3 T18; 4.1 T19; 5.2 T19; 5.3 T13–14; 6.1 T11–12; 6.3 T17	Comparison of two versions of two biographies, assessing the viewpoint of the writer.	50
Missing persons, page 71					
Listen, summarize and question	To enable children to extract main ideas from information texts. To introduce children to the distinction between open and closed questions.	1a, b, c; 2b; 3 *Reading for information, level D*	3.3 T19; 4.2 T15–18; 4.3 T20; 5.2 T16; 5.3 T14, 16; 6.3 T17–18	Teacher demonstrates summarizing and questioning techniques.	52
Identifying current knowledge, page 52					

NON-FICTION

ACTIVITY TITLE	LEARNING OBJECTIVE	POS/AO	NLS	CONTENT	PAGE
Lexical cohesion in information texts	To help children to appreciate the role played by subject-specific vocabulary in establishing the reader's expectations about the nature of a text. To enable children to use expectations about the general nature of a text to arrive at the meanings of difficult words. To practise using a dictionary.	1a, b, c; 2b; 3 *Reading for information, level D*	3.1 W13–18, S2; 3.2 W17–22, S1; 3.3 W12, 15, S1; 4.3 T18; 5.1 W8; 5.2 W10, T15; 5.3 W12–13; 6.1 W10	Comparison of vocabulary from three texts on a related topic.	53
Underlining key words, page 55; Morphemic word-webs, page 121					
Comparing dictionaries	To enable children to practise using dictionaries and to become familiar with dictionary conventions. To develop critical awarenes of dictionary writing.	1a, b, c; 2b; 3 *As above*	3.1 W13–18, S2; 3.2 W17–22, S1; 3.3 W12, 15, S1; 4.3 T18; 5.1 W8; 5.2 W10, T15; 5.3 W12–13; 6.1 W10	Children compare efficacy of definitions of target words from a range of dictionaries.	55
Crosswords, page 120; Morphemic word-webs, page 121; Antiscrabble, page 123					
Information exchange	To enable children to extract main ideas and significant issues from information texts. To enable children to identify issues shared by texts and compare the treatment of such issues. To foster discussion and questioning of information texts.	1a, b, c; 2b; 3 *As above*	3.1 T20; 3.3 T19; 4.3 T16–18, 20; 5.2 T17; 5.3 T13–14; 6.2 T16; 6.3 T17	Children read related but different texts then interview each other on the content.	57
Generating questions, page 67; Role play, page 68					
Connectives	To raise children's awareness of the role of different types of connective in signalling relationships between sentences and paragraphs.	1a, b, c; 2b; 3 *Reading for enjoyment, level D*	3.3 S5, 6; 4.3 S4; 5.3 S6–7; 6.1 W4–5; 6.2 W8; 6.3 S1	Children compose continuations of a text given sentence and connective.	58
Paragraphing	To familiarize children with sentence sequences within paragraphs.	1a, b, c; 2b; 3 *As above*	4.2 T20, 24; 6.3 T21; 5.2 T13; 4.2 T19	Children reorder shuffled sentences into coherent paragraphs.	60
Sequencing, page 65					
Believe it or not	To enhance children's motivation to read a wide range of non-fiction. To provide a context for note-taking, non-fiction reviewing and referencing. To be aware of some of the ways in which authors record and acknowledge their sources.	1a, b, c; 2b; 3 *Reading for enjoyment, level D*	3.1 T21, 18; 4.2 T23; 5.2 T18; 6.1 T11	Children collect interesting facts and reference their sources.	62
Introducing writing frameworks, page 64					
What makes a poem a poem?	To develop awareness of the poetic aspects of language.	1a, c, d; 2b; 3 *Awareness of genre, level D*	3.1 T8; 4.2 T5; 6.2 T5	Children compare poetic and prose writing.	64
Shaping memorable language, page 88					

POETRY

ACTIVITY TITLE	LEARNING OBJECTIVE	POS/AO	NLS	CONTENT	PAGE
A community anthology	To raise awareness of the role that poetry and poetic language play in everyday life and in the memories of ordinary people. To create a class anthology of favourite poems.	1a, c, d; 2b; 3 *Reading for enjoyment, level C*	3.1 T3; 4.1 T7; 4.3 T7; 5.1 T7; 5.2 T7; 5.3 T6; 6.2 T5; 6.3 T2	Children collect poems from members of the school community.	66
Creating a place for poetry, page 76					
Dual-entry diary	To help children to select lines, verses or longer extracts from poems that they find particularly interesting. To record their reflections on these extracts in writing. To discuss their selections and reflections with other readers.	1a, c, d; 2b; 3 *Reflect on writer's ideas and craft, level D*	3.1 T8, 6; 4.1 T7; 4.2 T4, 5; 5.1 T7; 5.2 T6; 5.3 T5; 6.1 T3, 5; 6.2 T3–6. 6.3 T4	Children keep a journal in which they collect favourite pieces of poetry and their reflections on them.	67
Written responses, page 90					
Choral reading	To enhance children's awareness of the power of the spoken word in relation to poetry. To select, prepare and perform a poem.	1a, c, d; 2b; 3 *Reading aloud, level D*	3.1 T6; 3.2 T4–5; 3.3 T7; 5.2 T5; 5.3 T4	Children select and recite favourite poems, performing co-operatively.	68
Role play, page 92					
Learning poems by heart	To enhance appreciation of personally chosen poems. To develop confidence in public speaking. To learn a favourite poem by heart.	1a, c, d; 2b; 3 *As above*	3.1 T6; 3.2 T4–5; 3.3 T7; 5.2 T5; 5.3 T4	Children select poems to memorize and recite.	69
A personal anthology, page 96					
Mysterious poetry	To encourage individual reflections on poems. To enhance awareness of how writers create a sense of uncertainty in readers.	1a, c, d; 2b; 3 *Reflect on writer's ideas and craft, level D*	4.1 T7; 4.2 T4; 5.1 T7; 5.2 T10; 6.1 T3; 6.2 T3; 6.3 T4; 6.2 T6	Children reflect on and discuss personal interpretations of mystery poems.	70
Narrative poems	To enhance children's appreciation of narrative poetry through discussion, visualization and inference.	1a, c, d; 2b; 3 *Reading for enjoyment, level D*	4.1 T4; 5.2 T4; 6.1 T3; 6.2 T9	Children select, sequence and illustrate episodes from narrative poetry.	72
Graphic responses, page 91					
Metaphor	To make children more aware of the role of metaphor in poetic and other types of writing.	1a, c, d; 2b; 3 *Knowledge about language, level E*	4.2 T5; 5.1 T8; 5.2 T10, W12; 6.2 T3	Children discuss the meanings of thematic metaphors from 'Macbeth'.	73
Riddles, page 80					
Compounds, coinages and kennings	To explore the metaphorical aspects of morphology.	1a, c, d; 2b; 3 *As above*	4.3 W11, 7; 5.1 T8; 5.3 W12; 6.3 W5–7	Children analyse and invent compound words.	74
Antiscrabble, page 123					
From non-fiction to poetry	To help children to identify main ideas in a descriptive passage and the words and phrases that express them. To identify redundant words and phrases. To find similes, metaphors and related words and phrases to elaborate main ideas.	1a, b, c, d; 2b; 3 *As above*	3.1 T12, 20; 3.3 T26; 4.1 T17; 4.2 T13–14, 17, 21; 4.3 T14–15, 20; 5.1 T16–17, 23; 5.3 T16; 6.1 T18	Children transform information text into poetic form by editing and paraphrasing.	76
Onset and rime onomatopoeia generators	To enable children to practise blending skills by using a matrix to permutate onsets and rimes. To reflect on the aesthetic qualities of the words that they create. To engage in creative writing to assign meanings to these words.	1a; 2a; 3 *As above*	3.3 T6; 5.1 T8, W2; 5.2 W11; 5.3 W13; 6.2 T3–4; 6.3 W6–7	Children create and define new words by combining onsets and rimes.	77
Antiscrabble, page 123					

MEDIA AND MISCELLANEOUS

ACTIVITY TITLE	LEARNING OBJECTIVE	POS/AO	NLS	CONTENT	PAGE
A letter to the council	To consider the issues involved in communications between the public and official bodies. To consider letters written in order to complain. To understand the appropriateness of formal/informal style.	1a, b, c; 2b; 3 *Awareness of genre, level D*	3.3 T16; 4.4 T16–18; 5.3 T12–15; 6.2 T15–17; 6.3 T16	Children analyse an example of official correspondence.	79

It's a well-known fact, page 114

| Scramble | To recognize vocabulary and discourse choices which characterize different types of newspaper. To reflect on how this affects the conveyance of news and what it implies about newspapers' beliefs about their readers. | 1a, b, c; 2b; 3 *As above* | 4.1 T20–21; 4.3 T16; 5.3 T13–15; 6.1 T12; 6.2 T15–16 | Children identify distinct styles of writing in examples of mixed text. | 80 |

Anatomy of newspapers, page 108

| Newspapers now and then | To investigate the language of reporting and how it has changed through time. | 1a, b, c; 2b; 3 *As above* | 4.1 T20–21; 4.3 T16; 5.3 T13–15; 6.1 T12; 6.2 T15–16; 6.2 T19 | Children compare and discuss old and contemporary styles of reporting. | 82 |

Exploring newspaper articles, page 112

Text comparison	To explore the different perspectives on a topic that readers can gain through reading a variety of texts.	1a, b, c, d; 2b; 3 *As above*	3.1 T16–17, 19; 4.1 T16; 5.2 T15, 19; 5.3 T14; 6.1 T12, W7	Children compare four different genres on the same topic.	83
The register	To heighten children's awareness of the registers or text conventions that shape particular genres, and to explore the consequences of departing from these conventions.	1a, b, c; 2b; 3 *Awareness of genre, level E*	4.1 T16, 20; 4.3 T19; 5.3 T13–15; 6.1 T12; 6.3 T19	Children analyse adverts and horoscopes that break the rules governing the use of language in these texts.	84
Cards, lists and post-its	To investigate the conventions underlying everyday written messages.	1a, b, c; 2b; 3 *Awareness of genre, level D*	3.1 T19; 3.3 T16; 4.1 T16–17; 6.1 T12; 6.3 T19	Children collect and analyse a wide variety of ephemeral texts.	86

Junk mail, page 116

| International communication | To explore some possibilities for extending literacy afforded by the Internet and e-mail. To read and write in electronic media. To write to new audiences. To expand the range of texts read. To compare vocabulary and discourse styles. | 1a, b, c; 2b; 3 *Reading for information and functional writing, level D* | 3.1 T19; 3.3 T20; 4.3 T21; 5.3 T17; 6.1 T15; 6.2 T4; 6.3 T22 | Children conduct an Internet search for same-name communities and initiate contacts between schools in different countries. | 87 |
| Wordplay compendium | To arouse curiosity about word games, and to persuade children to engage in games at word, sentence and text level in order to enhance reading and writing skills. | 1a, b, c; 2b; 3 *Reading for enjoyment, level C/D* | 3.3 T6, 15; 5.1 T8; 6.3 W5–7 | Children collect, investigate and invent a wide variety of word games. | 88 |

Antiscrabble, page 123

| Creating clear instruction | To extract key information from an extended text. To recast information using the conventions of instructional text. | 1a, b, c; 2b; 3 *Reading for information, level D* | 3.2 T14, 16; 4.1 T22, 25–26, 5.1 T25 | Children take a piece of descriptive writing and recast it into instructions. | 89 |

Classroom manuals, page 98

| Ten years after | To encourage children to reflect on personal reading experiences and the pervasiveness of literacy in everyday life. | 1a, b, c, d; 2b; 3 *Reading for enjoyment, level D* | 4.1 T16; 4.2 T9; 4.3 T10; 5.1 T8; 5.3 T1, 14; 6.1 T3, 12 | Children collect examples of personally significant materials. | 90 |

Fiction

The aim of this chapter is to develop children's reading skills by providing a set of activities which exploit their curiosity about different types of narrative. The activities explore some of the ways in which narrative is structured at text and sentence level.

Readers are encouraged to identify, reflect upon, and in some cases to emulate in writing the devices through which writers capture the reader's attention and maintain his or her involvement in the narrative. The traditional 'story grammar' categories of setting, character and plight are explored, as well as smaller scale points such as vocabulary choice, dialogue and 'hook' sentences. Personal response to stories is encouraged through discussion activities which prompt readers to relate events to their own lives, and to make and defend moral judgements.

All of the activities involve discussion, and are based on whole stories or story fragments. These texts might be used as material for shared reading at the beginning of the Literacy Hour, while more focused follow-up work could occupy the guided and independent group work time. Ideas are also provided for more open-ended literacy investigations which can be continued beyond the constraints of the Literacy Hour.

FIRST SENTENCES

To enable children to anticipate the general content of a fictional text by reflecting on its opening sentence. To enhance critical awareness of the devices used by authors to draw readers into the text.

†† *Whole-class.*

🕐 *15 minutes.*

Key background information

This activity encourages children to reflect on one of the most common devices used by authors to motivate their readers: the captivating opening sentence. It also encourages children to reflect on their knowledge of text types and plot, and to practise the oral and performance arts involved in storytelling.

This is an activity which combines sentence-level and text-level work. It makes demands on children's oral ability, and it is probably best to try it out a few times during story sessions at the end of the day before attempting to incorporate it into the tighter timetabling of the Literacy Hour. When you and your pupils are accustomed to the procedure, however, it can make a very effective opening to the Literacy Hour. It can also provide the foundation for work at sentence level.

Preparation

Familiarize yourself with the opening sentences of a wide variety of novels and stories, and try to analyse what it is about them that would make a reader want to read on, or perhaps abandon the book. Think about the differences between sentences which are immediately enticing, and those which take a more subtle or deferred approach.

Practise this process, as you will be encouraging the children to engage in it also. Read the first sentence of a completely unfamiliar story, then close the book, reflect for a few minutes on how the story might develop, then recite your own continuation of the story, preferably using a tape recorder. Listen to your version then compare it with the published one. Think about the skills you have used in carrying out this activity and how you might help children to develop those skills.

Make a collection of stories and novels whose first sentences you think might be appropriate for the children you teach.

Resources needed

A selection of novels and short stories.

What to do

Introduction

Read a selection of first sentences out to the children. After each one, ask the children what kind of story they think is going to follow, and what will happen next. Ask the children to justify the responses that they make, and to assess how well the author appeals to the reader's desire to read on.

Development

Now demonstrate the main part of the activity to the children. Tell them that you are going to have a go at making up your own oral story from a first sentence. Take a book that you have not read and read the first sentence aloud. Close the book, think aloud for a couple of minutes, commenting on what you have read, then start telling your story. You need not go very far, just far enough to show that you have thought about what you have read and made some justifiable predictions. When you have done this, read the author's continuation and ask the children to compare it with your own. Which continuation did you prefer? How did my continuation compare with your own anticipations? What insights and emotions was the author trying to arouse with the first sentence.

Conclusion

Read another first sentence to the class and ask for a volunteer to go through the process you have demonstrated. It is vital that you give the child time to think about what might come next. When the pupil has finished his or her telling, ask the class to comment on it in the light of the stimulus sentence (try to ensure that the children's comments are constructive). Then read out the author's version and make comparisons. Repeat the process for as long as interest level and time permit.

Suggestion(s) for extension

The children's oral contributions can be used as the basis for written versions which might, if the children are sufficiently motivated, be expanded into full stories.

Children can also make collections of effective (and perhaps not so effective) first sentences, commenting on their assessments. Discuss the wisdom of judging a book by its first sentence, and encourage the children to think critically about books and stories which use lurid or otherwise 'obvious' strategies in their openings to entice readers.

Suggestion(s) for support

Children with limited experience of reading might find it difficult to make predictions, and those with limited oral confidence will be reluctant to join in with whole-class storytelling. In the first case, working from the first sentence of a familiar story is a good idea – retelling from the first sentence of a story that the children have heard read aloud would be ideal. From this reassuring start, try providing a starter sentence which offers a significant departure from the familiar story ('Little Red Riding Hood lived with her Grandma… on the very top floor of a block of flats in Plumstead').

Children who are reluctant to storytell in a whole-class setting might be less inhibited in a smaller group. The oral composing task might also be adapted to shared writing, in which the teacher writes down a continuation suggested by an individual or group. Another possibility for shy children is to ask them to draw a continuation of the story: these drawings can then be used as a set of prompts for later oral and written work.

Assessment opportunities

The children's contributions to oral storytelling can provide evidence of their developing skills in speaking and listening, while the content of their contributions in relation to the stimulus sentence can give some indication of their reading range and appreciation of literary language. However, it

would be a pity to overshadow the main purposes of this activity, which are to motivate and entertain through reading and telling.

Opportunities for IT

Pupils could be provided with a simple writing frame loaded into a word processor which consists of just the opening sentence. They could write the opening paragraph of their own story, possibly going on to write more if there is time.

Alternatively, the word processor could be used with a group during guided writing to demonstrate how to write and craft their own opening paragraph.

Display ideas

Starter sentences can be written at the centre of a story web, with illustrated written versions of a variety of continuations, including the author's, displayed on radii. Comments by the children on why they chose to continue as they did can also form part of the display. At a more sophisticated level, children can highlight portions of their continuations, and link these with threads back to the similarly highlighted elements which inspired them in the starter sentences.

Other aspects of the English PoS covered

Speaking and listening: 1a, b, c; 2a, b; 3a, b.
Writing: 1a, b, c; 2a, b, c, d, e; 3a.

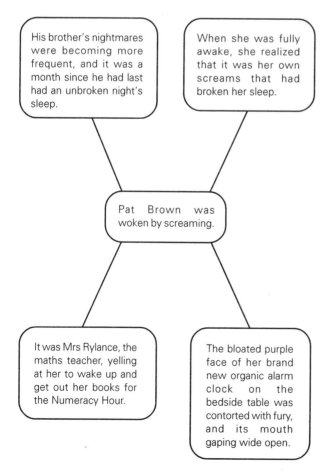

COMPARING VERSIONS OF CLASSIC STORIES

To familiarize children with significant stories from a range of cultures. To explore a variety of textual devices by which authors have presented their own versions of these stories throughout history. To encourage children to reflect on their own responses to these devices, and on their own literary preferences.

†† *Introductory reading during the first phase of the Literacy Hour, followed by group work during guided reading and/or independent work phases.*

⏲ *Two or more sessions of one hour.*

Key background information

This set of activities encourages children to reflect on classic stories and on how writers and publishers attempt to make these stories appealing to contemporary readers. The relevance of these stories, and the issues of authenticity and reverence towards them, might also be addressed. The activities might be linked to a historical theme on Greece or on the myths and legends of other cultures.

Preparation

Read the four versions of 'The Odyssey' referred to in 'Resources', and any other versions that you can find. Familiarize yourself with the stories if necessary. Try to sort out for yourself the major ways in which the stories differ. What age groups do they seem best suited to? Why? How do the vocabulary and the sentence structures differ? What role, if any, is played by graphics? Which version seems the most authentic to you? Why? Which seems the most accessible to children? Are there any anomalies or omissions in different versions of the same stories? Try to decide which is your favourite version and to identify the reasons for your decision.

Prepare writing frames for the children like the one shown here – one for each child. Make enlarged versions of the opening paragraphs of each of the books or cartoon frames; alternatively, do this for a particular episode (for example, the story of the Cyclops).

Episode

Version

Setting

How the writer tried to get me interested.

How this episode made me feel.

How the writing differed from the other version.

Resources needed

Copies of *Odysseus Goes Through Hell* by Tony Robinson and Richard Curtis (Hodder), *The Comic Strip Odyssey*, Diane Redmond and Robin Kingsland (Puffin), *Black Sails Before Troy* Rosemary Sutcliffe (Puffin), and *The Odyssey* translated by E. V. Rieux (Everyman), writing materials, writing frames as described in 'Preparation'.

What to do

Introduction

As a prelude to the activities below, read or tell some of the stories from '*The Odyssey*' to the children during storytime. Some of the stories are likely to be familiar to at least some of the children. Talk about the history of the stories and get the children to discuss why they think these stories have proved to be so enduring. Ask whether the children, or anybody they know, have had experiences which remind them of those in the stories.

If you are doing this activity as part of the Literacy Hour, read the paragraphs or look at the cartoon frames you have prepared during the whole-class opening phase, and ask the children to discuss the similarities and differences between them. Encourage children to focus on both the obvious differences (comic strip versus unillustrated 'epic' form) and more subtle features such as vocabulary and sentence structure. Ask the children to voice their preferences and to give the reasons for them.

Development

Encourage the children to investigate the different texts using the writing frames you have prepared. This investigation can be developed in various ways, depending on the age and ability of the children you teach, and the degree of flexibility with which your school is conducting the Literacy Hour. Possibilities are outlined below.

▲ A high-ability group conducts the entire investigation themselves. On different days they should read selected chapters from all four versions as independent activities, with one of the more challenging versions (Rieux or Sutcliffe) as a guided reading text. On the fifth day they share their opinions about the texts and complete the writing frame independently, discussing their findings with the whole class during the concluding plenary.

▲ Different ability groups read chapters from versions selected for their level of challenge. (For example, the highest ability group would read the Rieux, the lowest ability group the comic strip version.) This can be done either as an independent activity or as guided reading. At the end of the session groups could present their feelings about their particular version to the class. At the start of the next day's Literacy Hour, the range of texts is re-presented by the teacher who leads a more in-depth discussion of their similarities and differences. The children can then complete their photocopiable sheets during independent group work time.

▲ Groups are given two or more versions of the same chapter to read and discuss during independent group time. This will probably take more than one day to complete. When the work has been completed, groups can share their experiences and preferences with the class. Subsequent work can then follow the same pattern as in the second suggestion above.

Conclusion

Talk to the children about the issues raised by this work. For example, is there a danger of old stories getting 'spoiled' if people update them too much? Is there a greater danger of them getting lost if people don't update them? Relate this to the children's other experiences of multiple versions of popular stories. For example, Robin Hood, Winnie the Pooh, Hercules and Robinson Crusoe are all characters who have been updated through several versions in print and on screen.

Suggestion(s) for extension

Following on from the suggestions made in the conclusion, more able readers can search out and classify versions of popular hero stories, finding parallel versions of Robin Hood and Hercules stories, for example. At a more formal level, children can make analyses of the vocabulary and sentence patterns found in different versions.

For the former, they can make simple tallies of different word types used in a 100-word sample from each version; for the latter, they can count the number of words used in a given number of sentences from each version.

Suggestion(s) for support

Slower readers can be helped to gain access to the texts through shared and paired reading. The completion of the writing frame can also be done co-operatively.

Assessment opportunities

Note the children's awareness of textual features such as sentence complexity, vocabulary, the use of contemporary reference and of humour.

Opportunities for IT

The pupils could use a word-processed version of the photocopiable sheet as a writing frame; using the word processor to add, amend and edit their ideas for each version of the story. These could be printed out in larger text on to an OHP acetate for use by the children in the feedback session at the end of the series of lessons, or for display in the classroom.

Display ideas

An effective book display can be made of different versions of several stories. This can include material related to television and cinema versions. Graphic depictions of heroes like Robin Hood and Hercules in advertisements, cartoons and other aspects of popular culture can also be highlighted.

Other aspects of the English PoS covered

Speaking and listening: 1a, b, c; 2a, b; 3a, b, c.
Writing: 1a, b, c; 2a.

USING SHORT STORIES FOR GROUP READING DISCUSSIONS

To identify story themes. To discuss characters, settings and plots critically. To refer to and evaluate significant devices within the text. To compare and contrast authors and genres. To compare personal responses with those of other readers.

†† *A briefing on how this activity is to be conducted can be given to the whole class during story or circle time. Thereafter, the activity involves groups of four to eight children discussing their reading of short stories. This would be appropriate for the independent group work phase of the Literacy Hour.*

⊕ *20 minutes.*

Key background information

This activity is intended to help children to reflect more critically on their reading by providing them with a framework of questions to discuss before, during and after their reading of short stories. The framework is also applicable to longer works of fiction. Indeed, the questions which deal with character are likely to prove more fruitful with novels, in which the author has more space in which to develop this aspect of literature.

If your pupils are unaccustomed to this type of discussion, it is probably best if you introduce it to the whole class as an informal oral activity during story or circle time before attempting to incorporate it as a group work activity during the Literacy Hour.

Preparation

Select a short story that you think will hold the interest of the class. A list of promising authors could include: Susan Price, Joan Aiken, Margaret Mahy, Paul Jennings, Dick King-Smith, Jan Mark, Michael Rosen. Alternatively, you could use one of the stories from the photocopiable sheets in this book (though these are unlikely to be helpful with the questions related to character). Read the story yourself, then think your way through the questions in 'What to do'.

Resources needed

Multiple copies of a variety of short stories. The questions outlined in 'What to do'.

What to do

Introduction

Explain to the children that on some occasions in the future, different groups are going to be reading the same story, either together at school or individually as homework or during quiet reading time. After they have read the stories you will be asking them to share their opinions, using a range of questions as prompts.

To demonstrate this process, select a short story that you think would appeal to your class. Give the title of the story and, if you think it is appropriate, read the first sentence or two before posing the first set of questions. Try to accept children's responses to these without being judgmental either positively or negatively; aim to create a sense of uncertainty about what is to come next. Start to read the story, then pause in your reading at a strategic point and ask the second set of questions. Then read to the end and afterwards show them the final questions, or your adaptations of them, on a poster or on the board.

Prompt questions
Before reading
What might this story be about? How do you know? Would you choose to read a story with this title/beginning yourself? Why? Why not?

During reading
Were you right in your hunches about what the story was likely to be about? How do you feel about it now? Is this story reminding you of any other story, or of anything that has actually happened to you, or to somebody you know or know about? What do you think might happen next? How do you think this story might end?

After reading
How did this story gain your attention at the beginning? (If it didn't gain your attention, why not?) How did it make you feel at the end? Who wrote this story, and where do you think he or she got their ideas from? What issues or problems do you think the author wanted to make you think about, and/or how did the author want to make you feel? Could this story be true? How do you know? What did you think about the characters? Was there anybody you particularly liked, or disliked, or identified with, or felt sorry for? Do you think that the author wanted you to like or dislike particular characters. How did he or she attempt to do this? When and where was the story happening? How is this different from here and now? Could this story happen here and now? Has anything that happened in the story ever happened to you, or anybody you know? What other stories, real or fictional, does this story remind you of? Do you think that this is a good story? Why? Why not? NB. The vagueness of these questions, particularly the final ones, are intended to encourage a diversity of responses.

Development
Assign short stories which you consider to be suitable to the age and ability level of the children to groups of readers. Provide each child with a copy. The reading can be done either in school or at home according to circumstance. Very short stories could even be read within the Literacy Hour. During the group work section of the Literacy Hour, ensure that the children devote individual time to all three sets of questions, and that they share their responses after the story has been read.

Conclusion
Children can share individual and group responses to the questions during the final plenary of the Literacy Hour. To ensure that this is relevant to the rest of the class, the stories on which the discussions have been based should be familiar to the whole class, or the children's opinions should be presented in the form of a recommendation, giving reasons why the other children should or should not read the stories in question.

Suggestion(s) for extension
The discussions can form the basis for written book or story reviews, and children can contribute towards more extended written work evaluating particular genres or authors.

Suggestion(s) for support
Use the questions as the basis for discussion during guided group reading.

Assessment opportunities
Note the children's ability to formulate, express and adapt ideas, deal with opposing points of view, identify themes and significant details in their reading, and respond to fiction critically and imaginatively.

Opportunities for IT
Those children carrying out the extension activities could use a word processor with a writing frame created from a sub-set of the questions explored during the reading time. This would help to guide the children's writing of a book review. An alternative set of questions could be used as a word-processed writing frame to provide a structure for simple reviews which can be displayed in the classroom.

Display ideas
Concise written comments expressing a range of different opinions can form part of a display about particular authors or genres.

Other aspects of the English PoS covered
Speaking and listening: 1a, b, c, d; 2a, b; 3a, b.

DERIVING WORD MEANINGS FROM CONTEXT

To infer the meaning of unknown words from context and to generate a range of possible meanings. To use dictionaries to learn or check the definitions of words. To write their own definitions of words.

†† *Whole class followed by guided or independent groups.*

⏲ *15–30 minutes with the whole class during whole-text and focused-word work; 20 minutes group work.*

Key background information

This activity encourages children to think about the meanings of words by considering possible meanings suggested by the context in which they occur. It also encourages them to consult a dictionary to check their hypotheses rather than just looking up the word before they have attempted to work out the meaning. Children are also encouraged to consider what is involved in choosing a particular word to use in a story (rather than a near synonym) and about the effects on the reader of the author's choice of vocabulary. This activity combines word- and text-level work. The process of deducing meaning from context can be demonstrated to the whole class during shared reading, and this specific activity could be done by a small group during reading and writing time.

Preparation

Think about the vocabulary used by some of your own favourite authors or in publications that you read. What are your own reactions to the use of technical terminology, 'trendy' or exotic words? Look through your pupils' written work and select examples which show the effects of using both ambitious and down to earth vocabulary; alternatively, or in addition to this, select such examples from published material. Make an enlarged copy of photocopiable page 92. Make individual copies of photocopiable page 93.

Resources needed

Examples of writing as mentioned in 'Preparation', photocopiable pages 92 and 93, dictionaries, writing materials.

What to do

Introduction

Introduce the activity by talking about choices of vocabulary in fiction or, for example, newspaper reporting, and illustrate this by reading out some examples or the children's own examples which you have selected. (At a very simple level, you could compare the sentences: *He was chased by a big dog* and *He was pursued by an enormous hound*.) Try not to equate more unusual vocabulary with better writing.

Present your enlarged copy of the story from photocopiable page 92 and read it through with the class. You could do this by disclosing the story paragraph by paragraph and asking the children to predict what comes next. (This can be done both for this and subsequent activities by moving a mask down the enlarged version of the story, or by cutting the enlarged version into paragraphs and presenting them one at a time.) When the story has been read, discuss it with them, then ask them to identify any emboldened words from the first paragraph with which they are unfamiliar. Ask the children to speculate on possible meanings, and to justify their suggestions by referring to the surrounding context. Check the children's suggestions by consulting a dictionary, demonstrating how this should be done if necessary. (If the children already know the meanings of the words, ask them how they know that they have been used appropriately.)

Development

During group work time, children can complete the activity using photocopiable page 93. This requires them to write down possible meanings for each word and then to check their suggestions in the dictionary. Encourage the children to think about the effect on the story of substituting simpler synonyms for the more unusual vocabulary.

Conclusion

Children who have completed this activity can read alternative versions of the story to the class, using the synonyms they have identified. Ask the class which versions they prefer.

Suggestion(s) for extension

This activity should form part of regular work on vocabulary development and critical awareness of writing styles. You may want to share with the class George Orwell's recommendation that a writer should never use a long or exotic word if a shorter or more common one is available. Ask the children to challenge this by finding examples of the appealing use of unusual words.

Suggestion(s) for support

Give support by conducting the group work as a guided reading activity. Some children may benefit from a sentence-based 'guessing game' activity in which they think of meanings for an unknown word. The mock headlines suggested here may provide a starting point.

Polar explorers injured as sled hits sastrugi.

Too many weddings! Doctors blame tintinnabulation for vicars' hearing problems.

Magician turned into toad: inexperienced famulus blamed.

Tsunami washes away six towns on Australia's east coast.

Terror defeated: former arachnophobe now runs tarantual farm.

New design crash helmet offers improved cranial protection.

Neighbour's pet pigs inflict olfactory torture, residents claim.

It is important to note, however, that for each of these examples many different inferences are possible. As with the main activity, the idea is to get children thinking, and to use the dictionary to check their own hypotheses.

Assessment opportunities

Note the children's ability to use inference and to explain their thinking by making specific references to details of text. The efficiency with which children use dictionaries should also be observed.

Opportunities for IT

Individuals, pairs or small groups could use a word-processed version of the story in which each of the specific words is highlighted in colour or a different font style. They could then replace each of the synonyms with a word of their own. Once finished, they could print out their version to share with the class at the end of the lesson. The different versions could be used for display in the classroom for comparative work.

If the word processor used has access to a dictionary or thesaurus, pupils could be shown how to look up the highlighted words to check their meaning, or use the thesaurus to find an alternative word.

Other aspects of the English PoS covered

Speaking and listening: 1a, b, c; 2a, b; 3a, b.
Writing: 1a, b; 2a; 3a.

Reference to photocopiable sheets

Photocopiable page 92 provides a short ghost story in which unusual or difficult words have been highlighted. Photocopiable page 93 is for the children to complete after they have read the story. They are required to write down what each word might mean before checking their hypotheses in a dictionary.

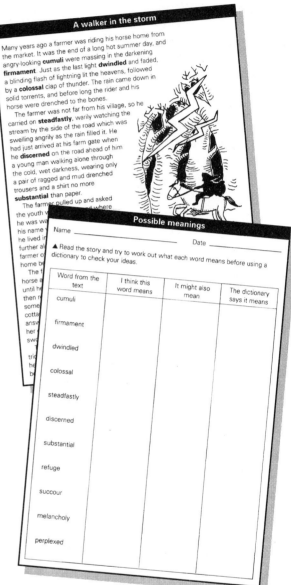

A walker in the storm

Many years ago a farmer was riding his horse home from the market. It was the end of a long hot summer day, and angry-looking **cumuli** were massing in the darkening **firmament**. Just as the last light **dwindled** and faded, a blinding flash of lightning lit the heavens, followed by a **colossal** clap of thunder. The rain came down in solid torrents, and before long the rider and his horse were drenched to the bones.

The farmer was not far from his village, so he carried on **steadfastly**, warily watching the stream by the side of the road which was swelling angrily as the rain filled it. He had just arrived at his farm gate when he **discerned** on the road ahead of him a young man walking alone through the cold, wet darkness, wearing only a pair of ragged and mud drenched trousers and a shirt no more **substantial** than paper.

The farmer pulled up and asked the youth …

Possible meanings

Name _____ Date _____

▲ Read the story and try to work out what each word means before using a dictionary to check your ideas.

Word from the text	I think this word means	It might also mean	The dictionary says it means
cumuli			
firmament			
dwindled			
colossal			
steadfastly			
discerned			
substantial			
refuge			
succour			
melancholy			
perplexed			

TSUNAMI washes six towns on Australias East Coast

VOCABULARY CHOICES IN FICTION

To familiarize readers with the vocabulary typical of fictional genres, and with the effects of departing from typical patterns.

†† *Whole-class introduction, followed by group work.*

🕐 *15 minutes introduction; 15 minutes group work.*

Key background information

Much of the 'texture' of a particular genre is provided by its vocabulary; as competent readers we almost automatically expect that certain words are more likely to occur in, for example, a ghost story than in a humorous story about animals. Inexperienced readers may lack such expectations, but if they can be familiarized with the idea that the content of a text implies a certain degree of predictability, then the burden of processing the words might be reduced for them. This activity might also encourage more accomplished readers to become aware of the cohesive influence of predictable vocabulary, and to play about with the effects of breaking textual expectations.

Preparation

Collate lists of words and phrases which you think are typical of specific story types (for example, a detective story might include the items fingerprints, clue, scene of crime, evidence). Make copies of photocopiable pages 94–95, one for each child, plus an enlarged copy for use with the class.

Resources needed

Photocopiable pages 94–95, lists of words and phrases specific to various literary genres, writing materials.

What to do

Introduction

Present your word lists to the class and ask them to try to identify what sort of story might contain such words and phrases. From their responses and explanations, try to establish the idea that specific types of story are likely to have predictable vocabulary in them, but that there is no inevitability about this. Using your enlarged copy of photocopiable pages 94–95, show the class the first three or four lines (the rest of the text should be covered up).

Ask them what type of story this appears to be. What clues did they use to draw their conclusions? For instance they may have noted that 'Once upon a time' usually signals the beginning of a fairy story which is a traditional tale. Conduct a shared reading in which the children provide suggestions for filling in the first few deletions, justifying their offers with reference to semantic and syntactic cues provided by the text. For example, 'wise, old _____ who...': the syntax says it has to be a noun while the semantics suggest something such as 'sage', 'king', 'wizard'. Continue the shared reading to the end of the text, prompting the children to say the word 'blank' or simply to pause whenever a deletion occurs in order to familiarize them with the text.

Development

A group of beginner or less experienced readers can then continue with this activity, using individual copies of the photocopiable sheet and preferably working in pairs so that different possibilities are thrashed out in discussion. When they have completed the task, they can compare their versions with other pairs of readers.

A group of more confident readers can be asked to complete the same activity orally, then to go back to the beginning of the text, and to work through it supplying responses which are syntactically appropriate, but not in keeping with the fairy tale genre. For example, a conventional completion of the first paragraph would probably produce the following sequence of words: king, daughters, beautiful, lovely, princes, marry. An unconventional completion might produce: accountant, customers, wealthy, stupid, conmen, swindle. However, the latter choices would set up a narrative thread that it would be very difficult indeed to sustain throughout the passage. The challenge for this group is to produce an alternative narrative which fits the remaining text but still undermines the expectations set up by it.

Conclusion

Ask the groups to read their completed versions to the rest of the class. The versions composed by the second group might arouse some hilarity or puzzlement. Try to get the children to appreciate the anomalies which underlie these reactions.

Suggestion(s) for extension

Capable readers can work in pairs preparing deletion passages for each other using extracts from different prose genres. Advise them to begin by making no more than one deletion in every ten words, and encourage them to experiment with supplying congruous and incongruous substitutions, in each case adhering to proper syntax.

Confident writers can be given sets of related words and asked to build a coherent text around them. A more challenging extension is to give readers a set of nonsense words with suggestive sound qualities. The children then have to assign meaning to these words in order to create a text.

Suggestion(s) for support

This type of activity is best supported by an oral cloze procedure, in which the teacher reads the whole passage aloud, saying 'blank' at each deletion. Possibilities for the gist of the passage are then discussed, and the passage read again, the children this time saying aloud their suggestions for the blanks and justifying their choices by referring to the meaning cues in the text.

Assessment opportunities

Children's responses to this type of activity should provide evidence of their familiarity with genres, and with their ability to use meaning cues and background knowledge in order to make appropriate suggestions for filling deletions.

Opportunities for IT

When the children have decided on the replacements for the missing words they could use a word processor to insert them into a copy of the text. They could use some type of formatting, for example bold, underline or italic, or other fonts or colours to make their own insertions stand out. These could be included as part of the class display.

A text disclosure program such as Topologika's *Sherlock* could also be used to give pupils experience in deciding which words are missing from the text. This software provides pupils with a copy of the text in which the teacher has deleted specific words. The children can work as a group to decide from the contextual clues what the missing words are. Guesses are discouraged by the use of a simple scoring system. The collaborative nature of a small group working together can generate excellent discussion on the possibilities for each missing word.

Display ideas

The children can illustrate their different versions of the story and these can then be displayed.

Other aspects of the English PoS covered

Speaking and listening: 1a, b, c, d; 2a, b; 3a, b.
Writing: 1a, b, c; 2a; 3a.

Reference to photocopiable sheets

Photocopiable pages 94–95 provide what seems to be a traditional fairy story but with a number of words deleted. The children attempt to fill in appropriate words using the semantic and syntactic clues offered by the text and their knowledge of the genre. The text with appropriate words filled in is given opposite.

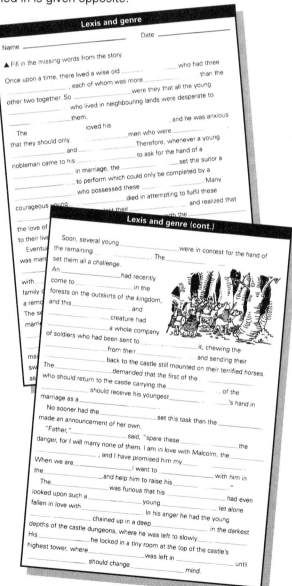

Once upon a time, there lived a wise old **king** who had three **daughters**, each of whom was more **beautiful** than the other two together. So **lovely** were they that all the young **princes** who lived in neighbouring lands were desperate to **marry** them.

The **king** loved his **daughters**, and he was anxious that they should only **marry** men who were **brave**, **wise** and **strong**. Therefore, whenever a young nobleman came to his **castle** to ask for the hand of a **daughter** in marriage, the **king** set the suitor a **task** to perform which could only be completed by a **man** who possessed these **qualities**. Many courageous young **men** died in attempting to fulfil these **tasks**. Others lost their **courage** and realized that the love of a beautiful **princess** was not worth the **danger** to their lives.

Eventually, the **king**'s oldest **daughter** was married to a **prince** who earned **her** hand by **slaying** with **his** bare hands a whole family of **dragons** who had **terrorized** a remote area of the kingdom for generations. The second eldest **daughter** was married to a **prince** who succeeded in **capturing** alive an immense **sea-serpent** which had been haunting the main **port** of the kingdom, swallowing **ships** whole as they approached the **harbour**.

Soon, several young **men** were in contest for the hand of the remaining **daughter**. The **king** set them all a challenge. An **ogre** had recently come to **live** in the forests on the outskirts of the kingdom, and this **loathsome** and **ferocious** creature had **slaughtered** a whole company of soldiers who had been sent to **kill** it, chewing the **flesh** from their **bones** and sending their **skeletons** back to the castle still mounted on their terrified horses. The **king** demanded that the first of the **suitors** who should return to the castle carrying the **head** of the **ogre** should receive his youngest **daughter**'s hand in marriage as a **reward**.

No sooner had the **king** set this task than the **daughter** made an announcement of her own.

"Father," **she** said, "spare these **men** the danger, for I will marry none of them. I am in love with Malcolm, the **swineherd's apprentice**, and I have promised him my **hand**. When we are **married** I want to **live** with him in the **woods** and help him to raise his **pigs**."

The **king** was furious that his **daughter** had even looked upon such a **humble** young **man**, let alone fallen in love with **him**. In his anger he had the young **apprentice** chained up in a deep **hole** in the darkest depths of the castle dungeons, where he was left to slowly **starve**. His **daughter** he locked in a tiny room at the top of the castle's highest tower, where **she** was left in **solitude** until **she** should change **her** mind.

OPENING PARAGRAPHS

To identify the genre of a story by attending to significant details in the text. To explore the expectations that are set up in opening paragraphs. To focus attention on how paragraphs are structured.

†† *Whole-class introduction followed by guided or independent group work.*

⏱ *15–30 minute introduction followed by 20 minutes group work. Suggestions for a more extended follow-up are included.*

Previous skills/knowledge needed
It would be helpful if the children had already completed the activity 'First sentences' on page 13.

Key background information
This activity encourages children to compare story settings and different styles of traditional story language. Children's attention is also drawn to sentence structure and the way in which paragraphs are organized.

The prediction activity in the introduction would fit into the opening 15 minutes of shared reading. The development could be carried out as a guided reading and writing activity.

Preparation
Make an enlarged copy of photocopiable page 96.

Resources needed
Photocopiable page 96, large sheets of paper, marker pens, board/flip chart, writing materials, paper.

What to do
Introduction
If you have previously carried out the activity 'First sentences' on page 13, refer back to the work you did and revise it by reading out a few opening sentences and asking the children to discuss what might happen next. Explain to the class that they will be looking in more detail at story openings and prediction.

Select one of the stories from photocopiable page 96 and, using your enlarged copy, read the first paragraph with the class, using a mask to hide the rest of the passage. Ask the children what types of events are likely to happen next, and what types of characters are likely to appear in the story. Encourage the children to justify their contributions by referring to the text itself and to any related reading or listening that they have done previously. Use this as a basis for introducing the term 'genre' if the children are not already familiar with it.

When the children have made predictions from the first paragraph, continue this process with the next one. This can be done as an oral activity with the whole class or as a group activity for guided or independent reading. If time permits, repeat the activity with a different story, or do this on a subsequent day.

Development

When the prediction activity has been completed, ask the children to look at each of the paragraphs in turn, and to try to identify what job each of them does in relation to the story, for example, introducing characters, creating suspense, setting up a problem. (Some of the questions posed in the activity 'Deriving word meanings from context' on page 19 might be useful here.) You could demonstrate this by taking the first paragraph, asking what it tells the reader, then writing down the children's responses and highlighting the appropriate phrase or sentence within the paragraph.

Direct the children's attention to the length of the sentences within each paragraph. A good way to do this is to use a large sheet of paper in order to write each of the sentences on a separate line. Discuss whether or not the length of a sentence has an effect on the reader. What about a succession of short or long sentences? Does a variation of sentence lengths help to hold the reader's attention?

Conclusion

Ask the children to write one or more paragraphs continuing and, if appropriate, concluding the story. Encourage them to make choices about what will be included in each paragraph, and about the length of sentences that they will use. Also mention vocabulary needing to fit in with the genre. Alternatively, ask them to write as freely as possible, and return to the completed story in order to make these choices retrospectively and so work on paragraph structure redrafting.

Creative work based on this activity can be shared with the rest of the class during storytime or a plenary session at the end of the Literacy Hour.

Suggestion(s) for extension

Encourage children to collect effective opening paragraphs and to analyse them in the way outlined above. They can also practise writing opening paragraphs in different genres, perhaps working under a wordage constraint in order to focus attention on sentence length and economy of language (say, no more than 50 words). A more challenging idea is to take paragraphs from the middles and ends of stories and to try to reconstruct what must have occurred and what might have occurred in the story already. This can be a very effective creative writing activity as well as teaching children about narrative structure and cohesive links between sentences and paragraphs.

Suggestion(s) for support

The procedures outlined above can be introduced informally as part of routine discussion during storytime. Some children may find the paragraph analysis tasks easier if you use stories with which they are familiar, though this will, of course, defuse the prediction element.

Assessment opportunities

Note the children's ability to identify elements of narrative and how these are conveyed through the organization of sentences and paragraphs.

Opportunities for IT

Children carrying out the extension activity may like to write their opening paragraphs on a word processor. They will then be able to use the word-count facility to check whether they have stayed within the specified amount.

Display ideas

A starter paragraph can form the centre of a spider web type display, with different continuations radiating out from it. Paragraphs can be displayed accompanied by annotations related to their place in the narrative, with appropriate phrases and sentences highlighted.

> Talking to nuts is a habit I learned from my grandma, who lived in a hazel-wood near Stonehenge.

> I'm going to tell you why I never crack a nut these days without talking to it first to see if anybody is inside. You probably think I'm a nut myself for doing this. Perhaps I am.

> Talking to nuts is not my only odd habit. I also wear odd shoes to match my odd feet.

> It all began when I heard my best conker scream with pain when it was finally split by my mate's champion.

Children could also be given one of the story openings as a word-processed file and asked to edit it into a different style of writing, perhaps changing action to dialogue or description. This is an ideal way to encourage pupils to craft, rather than simply draft their writing.

Other aspects of the English PoS covered

Speaking and listening: 1a, b, c, d; 2a, b; 3a, b.

Reference to photocopiable sheet

Photocopiable page 96 provides both a short folk tale and a more contemporary story. The children first make predictions about what will come next in the stories and then analyse the paragraphs in greater detail.

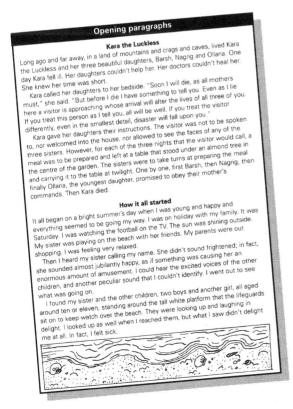

PREDICTION AND SENTENCE STRUCTURE

To become aware of grammatical devices which create expectations in the reader.

✝✝ *This can be done as a whole-class oral activity or as an oral and written activity during group or independent reading and writing during the Literacy Hour.*

🕐 *10–20 minutes.*

Key background information

This is a short sentence-level activity. You may find it useful to carry it out alongside the preceding activity 'Opening paragraphs'.

Preparation

Collect examples of sentences in which the writer uses a particular stylistic or grammatical device in order to signal an important development in a story. Some examples are given in the introduction section below. Depending on how you carry out the main activity, you may like to make copies of these sentences for the children to complete. For the support activity, prepare ready-made completions of sentences for the children to match to the sentence beginnings. (These can be either your own sentence beginnings or the ones provided below.)

Resources needed

The sentences provided below or examples of your own, board/flip chart, writing materials. For the support activity – completions of sentences.

What to do

Introduction

Read out a selection of incomplete example sentences. For instance:

▲ In spite of her promise to her father not to use the key,

▲ The bear showed its teeth; it gave a blood freezing snarl;

▲ It was a calm and quiet day, but

▲ Just as Ben was about to explain,

▲ Then I turned around the corner and

▲ As night was closing around them,

▲ Even as he reached the end of the trail,

▲ There, in the centre of the clearing,

Invite the children to complete them orally. Encourage the children to reflect on the fact that they are able to do this, even though they may be unfamiliar with the stories from which the sentences have been taken.

Development

Write two or three further examples on the board and ask the children to do the same thing again. This time though, ask children to identify the specific words in the sentence stem that signals what is most likely to come next. For example, 'calm and quiet' followed by 'but' signals that what follows is not going to be calm and quiet. 'Night closing around' signals thoughts of fear, or of cosiness. Introduce appropriate vocabulary as necessary. You may also like to point out examples of grammatical devices. For instance, the function of the conjunction 'but' in signalling a contrast or contradiction; the use of short clauses separated by semicolons (see the 'bear' example below) in order to build up suspense.

The activity can end here, or you can ask children to complete further examples as written work. You may like to hand out written copies of the sentences that you looked at in the introduction and ask the children to complete them.

Conclusion

Different completions for the same sentence stems can then be read to the class and their effectiveness discussed. Pay particular attention to completions which break the expectations set up by the first part of the sentence. (The bear showed its teeth; it gave a blood freezing snarl; then it sighed and ambled away into the forest.)

reading. You can also prepare ready-made completions for sentences such as those in the introduction, and get the children to match the halves of the sentences. Encourage them to talk about what it is in each half that signals their belonging together. Once the children are able to do this, they can be encouraged to formulate alternative completions both orally and in writing.

Assessment opportunities
Note the children's ability to identify the signals used by writers to create expectations, and their ability to create appropriate and imaginative completions.

Opportunities for IT
The children could use a word-processed writing frame from the sentences on the photocopiable sheet and then add their own endings to each of the sentences. Using a writing frame in this way reduces the amount of time needed for typing the first part of the sentences and helps children focus on the learning objectives of the activity. They could try out several different endings for each sentence.

Some children might find it helpful to use the computer to match the start of the sentence to an appropriate ending. If you use a word processor like *Textease* where the beginning and ending of sentences can be placed around the writing area, sentences can easily be moved around the screen so that the children can match the beginnings to the endings. It is also possible to set up two screens so that the beginnings are in one screen and the endings in another and the text dragged from one screen to the other. Similar activities can be created with other word processors.

Suggestion(s) for extension
Encourage children to generate several different completions for each sentence, including examples like the one above which break expectations. They can then try to locate examples of this device in their own reading. (Terry Pratchett's stories are a good source for this.)

Suggestion(s) for support
The best way to support this activity is to use it fairly frequently as an oral game during storytelling or story

Display ideas
Sentence stems can be displayed with a variety of congruous and incongruous completions, preferably created by the children, on movable cards. The children can then explore the effects of matching the different completions.

Other aspects of the English PoS covered
Speaking and listening 1a, b, c, d; 2a, b; 3a, b.
Writing: 1a, b, c; 2a; 3a.

TRACKING COHESIVE LINKS

To help readers understand how sentences and paragraphs in a narrative are structured and linked together.

✝✝ *Whole-class activity during the first part of the Literacy Hour, followed by guided or independent group reading.*

🕐 *15–30 minutes with the whole class, followed by 20 minutes group work during guided or independent reading and writing.*

Key background information

Cohesive links are words and phrases that are used to link a text together, giving it its 'texture' or underlying logic. This activity introduces children to this idea by focusing their attention on some simple examples of these links.

Preparation

Prepare a pseudo-text consisting of a dozen or so randomly selected and unrelated sentences put together in any order. Sentences culled from different pages of a newspaper would do. It might be enjoyable to commission a group of children to do this. Enlarge the pseudo-text as you will be using it with the whole class. Read through the pseudo-text and compare it with the first twelve sentences of a novel, story or report. Ask yourself what it is that distinguishes the real text from the concocted one. Also make a display copy of an extract of similar length from a story that the children are familiar with and will be able to read easily. Make copies of photocopiable page 97, one for each pair. For the extension activity choose some more demanding texts for the more able children to use.

Resources needed

One pseudo-text as discussed in 'Preparation', an extract from a story, photocopiable page 97, highlighter pens in a variety of colours. For the extension activity – more demanding texts.

What to do

Introduction

Display the enlarged story extract where all the children can see it and read the extract with the children. Allow time for them to discuss it, using the type of questions outlined in 'Using short stories for group reading discussions' on page 17. Now show the children the pseudo-text. Read through it with them and ask them to think about what makes the story extract more meaningful. They will probably be able to see that in the second passage the sentences do not form a coherent sequence: the sentences which follow the first one do not relate back to the theme of the 'opening' nor do they appear to share any theme at all. Refer the children back to the story and ask them to try to identify words and phrases which carry the theme from sentence to sentence. For example

Jim Fitt was the most agile boy in

South Rise Juniors. He often ran to school in the

morning, and when he arrived there, he would...

Development

Give out copies of the story starter 'A box of tricks' on photocopiable page 97 to pairs of children and ask them to read through it and discuss what it might be about. Then ask them to reread it and to underline in different colours the following words and phrases:

▲ those that are used to refer to the main character in the story

▲ those that refer to his sea chest

▲ those that relate to the sea and sailors

▲ those that are used to indicate a sequence of events.

The best way of organizing this is to give each task to two pairs of children. Pairs working on the same task can then compare their findings before all the pairs share what they have found.

As the children set about doing this, it should give you an opportunity to discuss with them:

▲ the use of pronouns to 'keep track' of characters without tedious repetition (the old man – he; a battered old sea chest – it)

▲ the substitution of different words, including synonyms and near synonyms, to add interest and variety (sea chest – box of tricks – that thing)

▲ the use of a group of words and phrases which are thematically related, sometimes very loosely, to maintain a particular atmosphere (docks, sailor, old salt, booming waves, seaweed, accordion, rum)

▲ different ways of indicating time relationships in the narrative.

Conclusion

Read out the families of vocabulary identified by the children to the whole class and ask them to try to guess what the story might be about. Recap the story starter with the class and ask them to think about finishing it.

Suggestion(s) for extension

As with sequencing, this type of activity can be applied to texts at any level of difficulty. Choose some texts that you feel would be challenging to the more able children in your class.

Suggestion(s) for support

Ask children who find this task difficult to identify the ten most important words in the story and to justify their choices. The story can be read to them, then cut into paragraphs and shuffled. Children can then be helped to reorder the story by identifying the clues outlined above.

Assessment opportunities

Note the children's awareness of the function of specific words and phrases in narrative, particularly the role of pronouns, and of relationships such as synonymy and semantic relatedness.

Opportunities for IT

The children could use a word-processed version of the story to highlight in different colours or font styles the words and phrases that relate to the different aspects of the story. Once this has been done the children could use the 'drag and drop' facility to pull all of these particular words together into a single list. They may need to be shown how to use the clip board 'cut and paste' tool to make this easier. These lists can then be used as the basis for further work with the rest of the class at the end of the lesson.

An alternative activity would be to ask the children to highlight in red the ten most important words in the story.

The ease with which the highlighting can be changed when using a word processor means that children can mark any key words to start with and then decide on the ten most important ones. The completed text can be printed out and used as a basis for further discussion about other groups' ten words. It can also be used as part of a class display.

Other aspects of the English PoS covered

Speaking and listening: 1a, b, c, d; 2a; 3a.

Reference to photocopiable sheet

Photocopiable page 97 provides a story starter. The children read through it and underline those aspects of the text which link the sentences and paragraphs together.

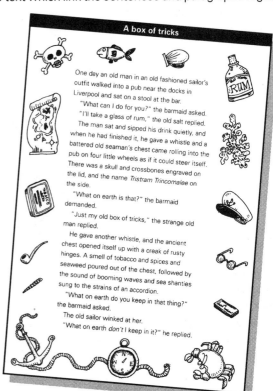

MISSING PIECES

To investigate the styles and voices of traditional story language. To identify typical story themes. To explore narrative order. To develop an active attitude towards reading. To understand aspects of narrative structure.

†† *Whole-class introduction followed by paired or individual work, then group work.*

🕐 *This activity should be completed within the appropriate periods of one Literacy Hour.*

Key background information

This activity encourages children to make creative inferences based on both their readings of a specific story and their more general knowledge of traditional story structure and human behaviour. The activity uses adaptations of two traditional folk-tales from which crucial details have been omitted. ('The poor man's dream' presents more of a challenge than 'The voices of the clocks'.) The children have to discuss what is implied by the rest of the story to make decisions about what is missing.

It is important that the children are reminded that they are not required to merely guess what was in the original version of the story, but to make a creative link which they can justify from their own reading. It is, however, a good idea to tell the children what was in the original version after the lesson, so that they can make comparisons. (In the original version of Jack's story, the pieman tells Jack that he dreamed of finding a pot full of gold coins under a dying apple tree in a muddy little garden; in the traditional version of Lola's story, the voices of the clocks chant that she is a thief.)

This activity also allows possibilities for vocabulary extension, either with the whole class during the second part of the Literacy Hour, or as an activity to be done during independent work.

Preparation

Make sure that you include plenty of traditional stories in your storytime, and that you talk with the children about typical themes running through such stories (adversity overcome, crime and punishment, perseverance and reward). Make an enlarged copy of either photocopiable page 98 or 99 for use with the whole class. Make copies of photocopiable pages 98 and 99, one sheet of each for each child or pair.

Resources needed

Photocopiable pages 98 and 99, writing materials, thesauri.

What to do

Introduction

Present to the children during the first phase of the Literacy Hour the enlarged text of whichever photocopiable sheet you have selected, using the gradual disclosure procedure recommended for prediction activities. Discuss the title first and encourage the children to think about possibilities for what the story might be about, then disclose the text a paragraph at a time, inviting predictions after each one. Try to focus the children on what is likely to happen in the next chunk rather than making guesses about the whole story. When you reach the first deletion mark, distribute the copies of the photocopiable sheet from which you are working and explain that you want the children to continue reading the story in groups. They must discuss what might

be missing, and reconstruct the story on their own or in pairs. It is important that they justify their reconstructions of the story by referring to the given information, and that they try to write with the same 'voice' as the given text. It is important to discuss this before they start to write.

If time allows, repeat this procedure with the other photocopiable sheet.

Development

The children can complete the activity in groups, working either independently of you, or as part of a guided writing activity.

If you are working with 'The voices of the clocks' story, ask the children to scan the text looking for words that are expressive of Lola's feelings of shame and fear after she has stolen the watch. Encourage them to offer related words from their own vocabularies or by searching thesauri. The children can then test the effects of substituting these new words for the ones given in the text.

If you are working with 'The poor man's dream' story, ask the children to search for words in the text which convey an impression of poverty and misery. In this case, they should be able to find nouns, verbs and adjectives. Again, encourage the children to find synonyms for these words and to test the effects of using them within the story.

Conclusion

During the plenary, children can read out and compare their reconstructions of the stories. If time allows, children who have been doing vocabulary extension can offer retellings of the story using their word substitutions. Also discuss style. How plausible are the children's suggestions? How well do they fit in with the children's experiences of the themes of traditional tales?

Suggestion(s) for extension

Fluent readers and writers can have a go at making up their own missing-pieces puzzles for partners, based on their reading of short traditional stories. Fables are a particularly good source for this type of work.

Suggestion(s) for support

The prediction and reconstruction can be done as a completely oral activity using the enlarged text. Children may find it helpful to carry out the writing aspect of this activity through shared writing.

Assessment opportunities

Note the children's ability to make inferences from what they have read. How plausible are their suggested constructions? The ability to share suggestions and to comment constructively on the ideas of others could also be noted. The ability to write in the style of a traditional story can also be assessed.

Opportunities for IT

The children could use a word-processed version of the story that has been prepared in advance and saved to disk. Once the children have decided how to complete the story they could type their ideas into the missing spaces and craft them to fit the style of the rest of the story. This new text could be highlighted in a different colour or font so that it is clear that this is the children's work.

Display ideas

Display different versions of the reconstruction of each story as friezes or as storyboards.

Other aspects of the English PoS covered

Speaking and listening: 1a, b, c; 2a, b; 3b.
Writing: 1a, b, c; 2a; 3c.

Reference to photocopiable sheets

Photocopiable pages 98 and 99 both provide traditional tales. However, an important element of each story has been omitted. Using clues in the text, and general knowledge of traditional story structure, the children attempt to fill in the omissions.

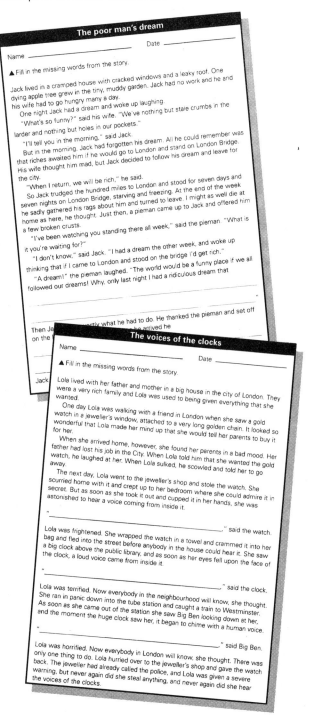

The poor man's dream

Name _____ Date _____

▲ Fill in the missing words from the story.

Jack lived in a cramped house with cracked windows and a leaky roof. One dying apple tree grew in the tiny, muddy garden. Jack had no work and he and his wife had to go hungry many a day.

One night Jack had a dream and woke up laughing.

"What's so funny?" said his wife. "We've nothing but stale crumbs in the larder and nothing but holes in our pockets."

"I'll tell you in the morning," said Jack.

But in the morning, Jack had forgotten his dream. All he could remember was that riches awaited him if he would go to London and stand on London Bridge. His wife thought him mad, but Jack decided to follow his dream and leave for the city.

"When I return, we will be rich," he said.

So Jack trudged the hundred miles to London and stood for seven days and seven nights on London Bridge, starving and freezing. At the end of the week he sadly gathered his rags about him and turned to leave. I might as well die at home as here, he thought. Just then, a pieman came up to Jack and offered him a few broken crusts.

"I've been watching you standing there all week," said the pieman. "What is it you're waiting for?"

"I don't know," said Jack. "I had a dream the other week, and woke up thinking that if I came to London and stood on the bridge I'd get rich."

"A dream!" the pieman laughed. "The world would be a funny place if we all followed our dreams! Why, only last night I had a ridiculous dream that

Then Ja... ...ctly what he had to do. He thanked the pieman and set off on the... ...he arrived he

Jack...

The voices of the clocks

Name _____ Date _____

▲ Fill in the missing words from the story.

Lola lived with her father and mother in a big house in the city of London. They were a very rich family and Lola was used to being given everything that she wanted.

One day Lola was walking with a friend in London when she saw a gold watch in a jeweller's window, attached to a very long golden chain. It looked so wonderful that Lola made her mind up that she would tell her parents to buy it for her.

When she arrived home, however, she found her parents in a bad mood. Her father had lost his job in the City. When Lola told him that she wanted the gold watch, he laughed at her. When Lola sulked, he scowled and told her to go away.

The next day, Lola went to the jeweller's shop and stole the watch. She scurried home with it and crept up to her bedroom where she could admire it in secret. But as soon as she took it out and cupped it in her hands, she was astonished to hear a voice coming from inside it.

"_____," said the watch.

Lola was frightened. She wrapped the watch in a towel and crammed it into her bag and fled into the street before anybody in the house could hear it. She saw a big clock above the public library, and as soon as her eyes fell upon the face of the clock, a loud voice came from inside it.

"_____," said the clock.

Lola was terrified. Now everybody in the neighbourhood will know, she thought. She ran in panic down into the tube station and caught a train to Westminster. As soon as she came out of the station she saw Big Ben looking down at her, and the moment the huge clock saw her, it began to chime with a human voice.

"_____," said Big Ben.

Lola was horrified. Now everybody in London will know, she thought. There was only one thing to do. Lola hurried over to the jeweller's shop and gave the watch back. The jeweller had already called the police, and Lola was given a severe warning, but never again did she steal anything, and never again did she hear the voices of the clocks.

PREDICTING FROM STORY ITEMS

To encourage children to generate hypotheses about the likely course of a story by reflecting on previous experience of reading narrative.

†† *Whole class, paired work, then whole class.*

🕐 *30–40 minutes.*

Key background information

Some researchers into reading comprehension claim that children bring understanding to their reading of new texts by linking ideas in the text with related ideas from their background knowledge of the world and their previous reading and listening experience. To facilitate this linking process, prior knowledge needs to be activated before the reading, so that readers are thinking along the right lines and have the appropriate areas of prior knowledge ready to help with interpreting the material to be read.

This activity presents a short and simple discussion routine, aimed at priming children's background knowledge and generating appropriate predictions, which can be integrated into storytimes and used on any occasion when children are approaching a new narrative text. This activity could be used at any time including, but not necessarily, the Literacy Hour. It would fit rather well into a traditional end of day storytime.

To exemplify the procedure, you will be using 'Anna's story', which is based on a traditional Scottish folk-tale. The story is also the starting point for the next two activities in this book, so this trio of activities with related follow-up work could be used as the basis for a week of literacy lessons.

Preparation

Make an enlarged copy of photocopiable page 100. Either find or draw some pictures of three or four items from the story; for example, a lonely hovel in a forest, a cloak of feathers, a weeping man, a happy family. For the extension activity gather together a set of pictures that relate to a particular genre of fiction. For the support activity make a collection of some pictures of items from stories with which the children are familiar.

Resources needed

Photocopiable page 100, pictures of some of the items mentioned in the text, writing materials, board/flip chart. For the extension activity – pictures relating to a genre of fiction. For the support activity – pictures of items from familiar stories.

What to do

Introduction

Explain to the children that they will be listening to a story, but before they do so, they will be engaging in some informed guesswork.

Show the children the pictures and tell them that the things depicted will feature in the story. (It is best not to indicate the sequence in which the items will occur.) Ask them what kind of story they think they will be listening to. Probe the responses in order to get the respondents to justify their guesses through reference to the pictures. It is likely that features such as the cottage and the cloak of feathers will elicit the idea of a folk-tale, but other responses might be justified as well. Then ask the children to discuss, in pairs, what might happen in the story, based on what thoughts and memories of other stories the featured items evoke in them. Give the children a good five minutes to do this.

Development

After the time-limit has elapsed ask two or three of the pairs to tell you what they think will happen in the story. Record these predictions using shared writing, at the same time encouraging the children to justify their ideas.

When two or three different versions have been recorded, start to read the story to the children. At strategic points, but not too often, pause and ask the children how the story compares with the predictions. Encourage the children to modify their predictions in the light of their listening.

Conclusion

When you have completed the story, ask the children how their predicted versions compare with the actual story. Talk about how their expectations were probably shaped by memories of previous stories that they had read, seen or listened to.

Suggestion(s) for extension

This activity can be modified into a stimulus activity for creative writing. Show the children a set of pictures typical of a particular genre of fiction; for example, a dragon, a knight, a princess; a footballer, a shady-looking character handing the footballer an envelope in a pub, the footballer in prison. Ask the children to compose appropriate stories, either orally or in writing, related to the pictures. In order to keep the pace of this activity brisk, you might find it advisable to impose a length or time restraint.

Ask the children to share their stories. When this has been done, set the children the task, perhaps for homework, of composing a completely different story based on the same pictures. The children can simply alter the events in the story or, more subtly, make it into a completely different kind of story. (For example, the dragon-knight-princess stimulus could become a crime story about a rare book of legends; or a soap opera episode about rivalries on a movie set.) Talk about how effective stories are often based on the thwarting of the reader's expectations about the story.

Suggestion(s) for support

Precede this activity by showing children pictures of items from familiar stories and asking them to identify the source. (For example, pictures of a farmhouse, a pig and a sheep-dog trial for *The Sheep Pig*.) The pictures related to this activity can then be used as the basis for a shared writing activity. When you have completed the children's own stories, read 'Anna's story' with the children and conduct a discussion on how their own predictions differed from or were similar to the events that they have just read.

Assessment opportunities

Observe how familiar the children are with ideas such as genre, expectations and the breaking of expectations. Note their ability to engage in critical discussion and co-operative composition.

Display ideas

'Anna's story' can be displayed alongside the children's compositions in a display centred on the pictures you used. You could also display another set of pictures as initial stimuli, and put up children's stories that have been inspired by them as they emerge.

Other aspects of the English PoS covered

Speaking and listening: 1a, b, c, d; 2a, b; 3a, b.
Writing: 1a, b, c; 2a; 3a.

Anna's story

Anna lived alone in a stone hut deep in the forest. Every day she had to gather wood for the fire, draw water from the stream, and pick whatever fruits and roots she could find growing wild in the forest. She had nobody to help her and nobody to talk to.

One day Anna was on her way to the stream when she heard the sound of somebody splashing in the water, so she hid in the bushes and tried to see who it was. She saw a young man climb out of the stream. He sat on a rock and began to sing in the most beautiful voice she had ever heard. Then he unfolded a bundle that lay nearby. It was a cloak of feathers. He put it on and instantly turned into a tiny, colourful bird. Then he spread his wings and flew away.

The next day Anna hid by the stream again. In the afternoon she saw a tiny colourful bird land on the rock. The bird fluttered a little, its feathers fell away, and Anna saw the young man standing on the rock. He folded up the cloak of feathers that lay at his feet and plunged into the stream.

Anna crept out of hiding, seized the cloak of feathers, and ran home with it. She hid it in the roof of her house. Then she waited until darkness was falling and walked back to the stream. The young man was sitting on the rock, but instead of singing he was weeping pitifully, and shivering.

Anna wrapped the young man in her own cloak and took him back to her house. She tried to talk to him but he could only weep and make cooing and singing noises. She looked after the young man for a long time. Soon he stopped crying and began to trust her. After much longer he learned to speak. After much longer again he and Anna fell in love and got married.

Anna's life changed. Her husband kept her company, sang beautiful songs to her, and helped her with all the hard work. Together they planted a garden around the house and grew flowers and vegetables. They had two children who grew up to be strong and healthy. The man seemed to be happy in the forest, but very often he would start to cry when he heard the birds begin to sing in the morning, or when he saw them flying south for the winter.

One day Anna went out with her older child to collect wood. When she came home she found that her husband had gone away. Her younger child, who was crying pitifully, told Anna that his father had found a cloak of feathers when he was fixing the roof, and that he had put it on and vanished. Anna never saw her husband again, but sometimes, when she was sitting in the garden with her children, a tiny colourful bird would flutter down and watch them very sadly.

Reference to photocopiable sheet

Photocopiable page 100 provides the text of 'Anna's story' which is adapted from a Scottish folk-tale. Using pictures of items from the story as a stimuli the children try to anticipate how the story will develop.

FOSTERING UNCERTAINTY – INFERENCES

To encourage readers to use inference and deduction in interpreting narrative text, and to compare, discuss and evaluate the different interpretations that they arrive at.

†† *Small-group guided reading with opportunities for whole-class discussion.*

🕐 *30 minutes.*

Previous skills/knowledge needed

It would be useful if the children had carried out the preceding activity 'Predicting from story items'.

Key background information

Deduction is the ability to draw specific conclusions from the statements explicitly provided in the text; inference is the process of using background knowledge to supply implicit information which is left unstated by the author. The processes are closely related and it is often difficult to distinguish between them. Both of them are essential active-reading processes, since no text gives the reader all the information that is required for comprehension. The reader has to supply connections based on background knowledge and previous readings.

The shared reading and discussion of the story can be done during the first 15 minutes of the Literacy Hour. The photocopiable sheet can be used during independent or guided reading and writing.

This activity is based on 'Anna's story' (photocopiable page 100), in which the connections between a sequence of events are left unstated. Readers are encouraged to use reflective reasoning in order to work out the most likely connections, but they are also encouraged to entertain alternative and less likely possibilities.

Preparation

Prepare an enlarged version of 'Anna's story' on photocopiable page 100 and make one copy of photocopiable page 101 for each two members of the group.

Resources needed

Photocopiable pages 100 and 101, writing materials, board/flip chart.

What to do

Introduction

Revisit Anna's story through shared reading, using your enlarged copy of the photocopiable sheet. At the points in the story indicated by the prompts on photocopiable 101, ask the children why they think that particular event occurred. Try to get the group to agree a response which seems most feasible, then challenge them to formulate alternative explanations. In each case, encourage the children to justify their responses by referring both to evidence that is explicitly stated in the text, and evidence derived from their own background knowledge.

Development

When you have completed the story, ask the children to summarize it orally. Ask the children to work with a partner and hand out copies of photocopiable page 101 for them to complete. Talk through it with the children, reminding them of the distinction between the most feasible explanation for an event and alternative possibilities.

Conclusion

Ask the pairs to compare their responses and assess the feasibility of any alternative explanations they may have decided upon. There may be opportunities to evaluate responses in the light of how the story actually developed. For example, 'If Anna stole the cloak of feathers in order to sell it, why did she hide it for years in the roof of the cottage?' This close comparison between uncertain speculations and the actual events revealed in the reading can lead to some lively discussion and to some very fruitful revisiting of the text.

Suggestion(s) for extension

This technique can be applied to any other narrative text. It also has great potential for the critical reading of non-fiction. Historical texts in particular lend themselves to this type of treatment. For example, children reading an account of the reign of Richard III can be encouraged to formulate alternative explanations for events such as the murders of the princes in the tower, at all times questioning accepted interpretations of events.

Suggestion(s) for support

The activity can be preceded or replaced by a purely oral game in which 'Anna's story', or a simpler one closer to everyday experience, is read out sentence by sentence. After each sentence the teacher poses the question 'Why?' Responses are taken and the two responses judged most interesting by the class or group are written down by the teacher. Subsequent sentences enable the group to evaluate their previous inferences and to refine their later ones.

Assessment opportunities

Note the children's ability to make judgements which combine careful reading with imagination and the use of background knowledge and previous reading experience.

Display ideas

The story can be arranged as a set of captioned pictures arranged horizontally. At each of the 'choice points' indicated on photocopiable page 101, an alternative

explanation can be represented as a branch leading off to another set of pictures which present a different completion to the story.

Other aspects of the English PoS covered

Speaking and listening: 1a, b, c, d; 2a; 3a.
Writing: 1a, b, c; 2a; 3a.

Reference to photocopiable sheets

Photocopiable page 100 tells 'Anna's story' which is adapted from a traditional Scottish folk-tale. Photocopiable page 101 requires the children to think about the story and reflect on why particular events may have occurred.

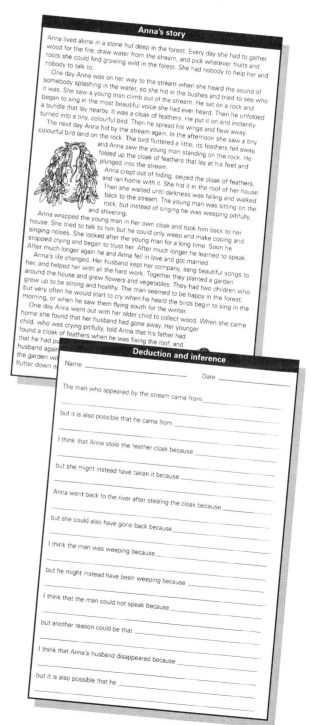

DEBATING ETHICAL JUDGEMENTS

To encourage readers to become more actively and empathetically involved in stories by encouraging them to evaluate the behaviour of characters.

†† *Whole class, then group work.*

🕐 *45–60 minutes.*

Previous skills/knowledge needed

This activity is best conducted after the children have completed the two previous activities 'Predicting from story items' on page 31 and 'Fostering uncertainty – inferences' on page 32.

Key background information

Reading fiction involves not just the decoding of print and the comprehension of ideas, but imaginative involvement in the lives of the characters who are depicted in the stories. Ethical judgements about the behaviour of characters is an inevitable aspect of such involvement. From their earliest experiences of literature, children distinguish between 'goodies' and 'baddies' and between 'happy' and 'sad' endings.

This activity is intended to make this process of identification and evaluation more reflective by getting the children to debate the rights and wrongs of a situation in which there is room for uncertainty about the morality of the characters' actions.

The shared reading and discussion of the story can be done during the first 15 minutes of the Literacy Hour. The photocopiable sheet can be used during independent or guided reading and writing.

Preparation

Prepare an enlarged version of 'Anna's story' on photocopiable page 100. If possible, try to obtain and read the story of the kelpie on which 'Anna's story' is based.

Resources needed

Photocopiable page 100, the kelpie story on which 'Anna's story' is based.

What to do

Introduction

Display your enlarged version of photocopiable page 100. Reread 'Anna's story' with the class, or ask one or two children to retell the story. Ask some questions which focus on the feelings of the characters, and encourage the children to try to identify with these characters. *How would you feel if you were Anna living on your own in the forest? How would you feel if you were a bird trapped in the body of a human being? How would you feel if a parent walked out of the house and never came back?* (You will have to be careful with the last question, as many children may have had precisely this experience.) After this discussion, pose the question: *Would it have been better if Anna had never taken the cloak of feathers?* Give the children five or ten minutes to discuss this question among themselves.

Development

Continue the discussion by asking the children to give their responses to the question, and to comment on each other's responses. Then divide the class into two or three groups: those who think it would have been better to have taken the cloak, those who think it would have been better to have left it, and those, if any, who are undecided. The 'ayes' and 'nos' should be given ten minutes in which to formulate two or three good reasons for their opinions. A spokesperson from each group can then present these reasons to the whole class. While they are doing this, anybody in the undecided group can go and join the ayes or nos depending on the persuasiveness of their arguments. At the end of the presentations, you can summarize the arguments before taking a vote on the question.

If time allows, repeat the procedure with the question: *Was it right for the husband to leave his family and return to the forest?* In order for this to be debated thoroughly, however, it might be advisable to postpone this to the next day, or to use it as the focus of a more informal discussion later in the day.

Conclusion

If you have managed to obtain the original version of the story, read it to the class and ask them to summarize the differences. The most obvious difference is that the seal woman has become a bird man. Ask the children to think about whether their responses to the debate would have been different in the context of the original story, given the gender shift of the two main characters.

Suggestion(s) for extension

The semi-formal debate procedure outlined in 'What to do' can be applied to any text in which there is an element of moral uncertainty. As with the preceding activity, it is also a useful technique for exploring and examining historical non-fiction.

Suggestion(s) for support

'Anna's story' can be approached through shared reading. The debate is a purely oral activity so should be accessible to all who have understood the story.

Assessment opportunities

Note the children's ability to engage in issue-focused discussion, to listen to contending points of view, and to base their ideas on clear reasoning.

Opportunities for IT

Children can create the two-column chart as suggested in 'Display ideas' below using a word processor or desktop publishing program.

Display ideas

Display the arguments for and against the key questions on a two column chart alongside an illustrated version of the story. The results of the vote, together with a summary of the issue debated, can be displayed below it.

Other aspects of the English PoS covered

Speaking and listening: 1a, b, c, d; 2a, b; 3a, b.

Anna's story

Anna lived alone in a stone hut deep in the forest. Every day she had to gather wood for the fire, draw water from the stream, and pick whatever fruits and roots she could find growing wild in the forest. She had nobody to help her and nobody to talk to.

One day Anna was on her way to the stream when she heard the sound of somebody splashing in the water, so she hid in the bushes and tried to see who it was. She saw a young man climb out of the stream. He sat on a rock and began to sing in the most beautiful voice she had ever heard. Then he unfolded a bundle that lay nearby. It was a cloak of feathers. He put it on and instantly turned into a tiny, colourful bird. Then he spread his wings and flew away.

The next day Anna hid by the stream again. In the afternoon she saw a tiny colourful bird land on the rock. The bird fluttered a little, its feathers fell away, and Anna saw the young man standing on the rock. He folded up the cloak of feathers that lay at his feet and plunged into the stream.

Anna crept out of hiding, seized the cloak of feathers, and ran home with it. She hid it in the roof of her house. Then she waited until darkness was falling and walked back to the stream. The young man was sitting on the rock, but instead of singing he was weeping pitifully, and shivering.

Anna wrapped the young man in her own cloak and took him back to her house. She tried to talk to him but he could only weep and make cooing and singing noises. She looked after the young man for a long time. Soon he stopped crying and began to trust her. After much longer he learned to speak. After much longer again he and Anna fell in love and got married.

Anna's life changed. Her husband kept her company, sang beautiful songs to her, and helped her with all the hard work. Together they planted a garden around the house and grew flowers and vegetables. They had two children who grew up to be strong and healthy. The man seemed to be happy in the forest, but very often he would start to cry when he heard the birds begin to sing in the morning, or when he saw them flying south for the winter.

One day Anna went out with her older child to collect wood. When she came home she found that her husband had gone away. Her younger child, who was crying pitifully, told Anna that his father had found a cloak of feathers when he was fixing the roof, and that he had put it on and vanished. Anna never saw her husband again, but sometimes, when she was sitting in the garden with her children, a tiny colourful bird would flutter down and watch them very sadly.

Reference to photocopiable sheet

Photocopiable page 100 tells 'Anna's story', adapted from a traditional Scottish folk-tale. In this activity the children use it to debate the moral stances of the characters.

To familiarize children with the distinctive types of language found on book covers, and to enable them to analyse this language critically.

†† *Small group working co-operatively.*

🕐 *20–40 minutes.*

Key background information

The covers and first pages of paperback books often feature uses of language which are intended to attract readers to the books. The analysis of this type of language can teach children a lot about the lexical and grammatical choices which underlie some forms of persuasive writing.

This activity would fit well within a scheme of work on media education. It can also be incorporated into book-making activities.

Preparation

Gather together a collection of paperback books, or photocopy some book jackets and analyse them in terms of the different kinds of language that are used, seeking out patterns in vocabulary choice, tense and layout.

Resources needed

Some paperback books or photocopies of book jackets, highlighter pens, writing materials, completed stories written by the children.

What to do

Introduction

Present the children with the paperback books you have collected and ask them to list all the different types of writing that they can find without even opening the books. The back covers of paperbacks are a particularly rich source of text types and children should be encouraged to pay particular attention to them. Then invite them to extend their search to the first few pages without looking at the story itself. Ask them to think about:

▲ how many different types of writing there are

▲ who wrote the different types of writing

▲ what the purpose of each type of writing is.

If you have made photocopies of the covers, the children can underline or highlight the different text types using a colour code, and write notes on each type directly onto the copy.

You may like to show them the example below to get them started.

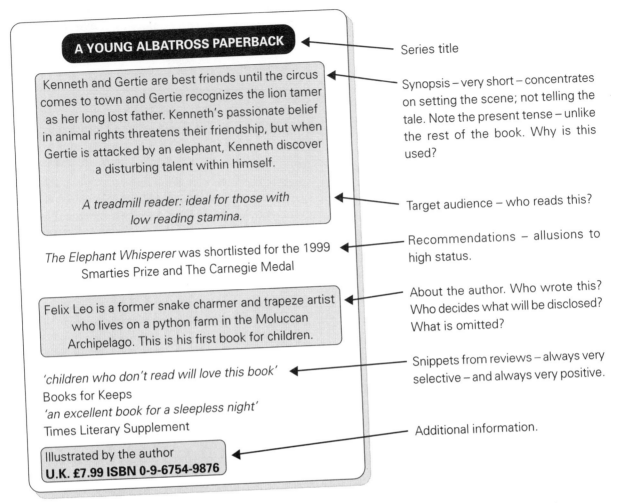

A YOUNG ALBATROSS PAPERBACK — Series title

Kenneth and Gertie are best friends until the circus comes to town and Gertie recognizes the lion tamer as her long lost father. Kenneth's passionate belief in animal rights threatens their friendship, but when Gertie is attacked by an elephant, Kenneth discover a disturbing talent within himself. — Synopsis – very short – concentrates on setting the scene; not telling the tale. Note the present tense – unlike the rest of the book. Why is this used?

A treadmill reader: ideal for those with low reading stamina. — Target audience – who reads this?

The Elephant Whisperer was shortlisted for the 1999 Smarties Prize and The Carnegie Medal — Recommendations – allusions to high status.

Felix Leo is a former snake charmer and trapeze artist who lives on a python farm in the Moluccan Archipelago. This is his first book for children. — About the author. Who wrote this? Who decides what will be disclosed? What is omitted?

'children who don't read will love this book' Books for Keeps 'an excellent book for a sleepless night' Times Literary Supplement — Snippets from reviews – always very selective – and always very positive.

Illustrated by the author **U.K. £7.99 ISBN 0-9-6754-9876** — Additional information.

Development
Make a diagram of the children's findings based on the example outlined above. Ask the children to think about the following points:
▲ why particular episodes are selected for the summary
▲ the summary writer's vocabulary choices (adjectives might be particularly telling)
▲ why the present tense is used
▲ who selects and writes up details about the author
▲ where quotes about the book come from and how these are collated
▲ who invents series titles and what the titles are based on
▲ what an ISBN number is for
▲ how book titles are chosen (a good opportunity to introduce the idea of intertextuality at a simple level).

Conclusion
Finally, refer the children to their own stories that they have written and invite them to write blurbs for them, incorporating all the layout and language features that they have investigated. Summarizing, composing quotes and mini-biographies provide opportunities for practising a range of grammatical and lexical skills. The children may find it easier to swap their stories and write the quotes and the mini-biographies for each other.

Suggestion(s) for extension
The technique outlined above can be applied to a range of media texts such as product packaging, junk mail and non-print media such as television and cinema trailers.

Suggestion(s) for support
Enlarge the photocopies of the book jackets and information pages and conduct the procedure through shared reading and writing.

Assessment opportunities
Note the children's attention to the less obvious aspects of the print environment, and their critical awareness of the origins and purposes of the features identified above.

Opportunities for IT
Those children carrying out the extension activity could use a word processor to write their own 'blurbs' for books they have read. They could be given a limited word count

and shown how to use the word count facility on their word processor. This will encourage them to craft their writing carefully.

An alternative approach would be to create a presentation using multimedia or web authoring software. They could include pictures that they have drawn using an art package. Alternatively, they could scan from their own line drawings or photographs. This kind of work requires careful planning over a series of lessons. The structure for the presentation can be set up in advance by the teacher so that the children can concentrate on the text, layout and messages of the presentation.

Display ideas
The children's own blurbs for their books can be put on display alongside enlarged and annotated examples from published books.

Other aspects of the English PoS covered
Speaking and listening: 1a, b, c, d; 2a, b; 3a, b.
Writing: 1a, b, c; 2a; 3a.

TIME PERSPECTIVES

To become aware of some of the ways in which authors handle the passing of time in fiction.
†† *Whole-class discussion and shared writing, with an opportunity for small-group follow-up.*
🕐 *30–40 minutes.*

Key background information
Children are invariably told that every story has to have a beginning, a middle and an ending. They are less frequently warned that events in the narrative are not always set out in chronological order. The majority of stories that children encounter in their early reading and listening do conform to the serial order of the traditional folk-tale, but much of the fiction that is written for older readers plays about with the sequencing of events. The use of flashbacks, flash forwards and dream sequences is common, as is the revisiting of events already described in order to redescribe them from different perspectives. (A 'flash forwards' is when the writer leaps ahead and describes the action as if from the point of view of somebody looking back on it.) This type of non-linear organization is also typical of the films and television narratives that children watch. This activity is aimed at raising children's awareness of this type of device by asking them to make a timeline of events that have been recounted in a non-linear order.

This activity is best suited to an extended reading, writing and discussion session outside of the Literacy Hour.

Preparation
Collect stories that are not told in linear order and have a

go at representing the events recounted using a timeline. (An interesting, classic, adult level example would be Robert Louis Stevenson's *Doctor Jekyll and Mr Hyde. Red Shift* by Alan Garner is recommended for older children.) Reflect on why the author has chosen to tell the story in this order. Make an enlarged copy of photocopiable page 102. If possible copy this onto an OHP transparency so that you can disclose the story section by section. Make copies of photocopiable page 103 – one for each child. For the support activity make sets of picture cards relating to each of the events on the photocopiable sheets.

Resources needed
OHP transparency of photocopiable page 102, photocopiable page 103, examples of stories told in a non-linear way, writing materials, OHP, board/flip chart. For the support activity – picture cards.

What to do
Introduction
Present the class with the enlarged version of the 'Goldilocks' story on photocopiable page 102. Disclose the story chunk by chunk, asking the children to guess what the story is. When the story has been identified, discuss the clues which gave the game away, then ask the children what differences exist between the traditional tale and this retelling. After discussing the dual perspective presentation, focus on the time element, and discuss why the author has chosen to begin with an event that happened almost at the end of the story.

Development
Next conduct a shared writing session with the children in order to continue and conclude the retelling of 'Goldilocks', maintaining the dual perspective narration and the use of flashbacks.

When this has been completed, ask the children to retell the story of 'Goldilocks' in its conventional form. Children can take turns doing this. As they do so, draw a timeline, indicating the order of occurrence of the events described. When they have finished, discuss the timeline and help them to construct a parallel line showing the events in the order that they occur in the unconventional retelling on the photocopiable sheet.

Conclusion
Discuss the use of flashback, flash forwards and dream sequences in fiction and in media such as television drama and cinema. Illustrate this with the examples of stories that you have collected. What is gained and lost by using these devices? Why are the devices used less in pictorial print narratives like cartoon stories? More accomplished readers can attempt time and narration lines for the more involved story opener that is presented on photocopiable page 103.

Suggestion(s) for extension

Encourage confident writers to try to incorporate different ways of handling time sequences in their own fiction writing. They can also be asked to make note of the use of similar devices in their own reading, and to assess the effect of them on the readability of the story.

Suggestion(s) for support

Help children to understand the difference between the order in which events are narrated and the order in which they occur chronologically by sequencing sets of picture cards as they read. For example, in the story 'The fugitive' on photocopiable page 103, you could make nine picture cards to represent the events that are mentioned in the passage. The children can arrange these cards as you conduct a shared reading, putting them in the order in which they are mentioned in the text, beginning with the author picking up his pen and ending with the orang-utan chasing Harry over the wall. The children could then revisit the passage and work out the order in which the events are supposed to have occurred. In this case, the first card will show the twins planting the apple trees, and the last card will show the author picking up his pen.

Assessment opportunities

Note the children's ability to distinguish between the order of narration and the order in which events occur in the stories.

Opportunities for IT

If your class has access to a large screen monitor or a projection device you could model the shared writing activity using a word processor. You might start with the key aspects of the Goldilocks story already prepared as a word-processed file and show the children how to move sections around into a different order (using the 'drag and drop' commands) and how to link these passages together, or how flashback sections can be worked into the text.

The same type of activity can be undertaken with a smaller monitor and a small group of pupils within a guided writing session of the literacy hour.

Display ideas

A simple display can be constructed from sequences of picture cards contrasting narration and occurrence sequences in stories that the children have read and written.

Other aspects of the English PoS covered

Speaking and listening: 1a, b, c, d; 2a, b; 3a, b.
Writing: 1a, b, c; 2a; 3a.

Reference to photocopiable sheets

Photocopiable page 102 is a retelling of the story of 'Goldilocks', while photocopiable page 103 is a story called 'The fugitive'. The children use these two texts to look at the ways in which the passage of time can be handled – namely, that events do not always have to be told in chronological sequence.

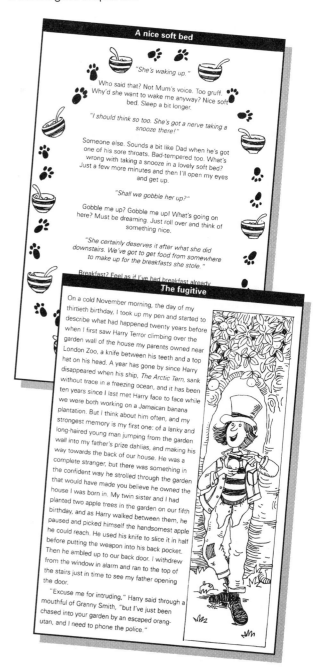

PREDICTING FROM SETTINGS

To understand how settings might influence events, atmosphere and characters' behaviour in stories. To understand how writers might play on readers' expectations in relation to settings in order to arouse curiosity.

†† *Whole-class activity followed by small-group discussion and writing.*

⏱ *40–50 minutes.*

Key background information

Our expectations about the meaning of what we read are conditioned by background knowledge, including previous experience of the subject matter through reading or other media. These expectations can be specific or general. Thus, the depiction of a setting which features a flat desert with monumental rock formations and tall cacti might evoke expectations of a Western adventure or a science fiction-type mystery, but is unlikely to evoke expectations of an inner-city school story. However, some authors create surprise and curiosity in their readers by deliberately undermining the expectations that their settings have created. This ploy is frequently used in comedy, most famously when a knight in armour walking along a rocky shoreline suddenly encounters a newsreader at a desk, announcing, 'Now for something completely different.'

This activity can be introduced to the whole class during the first 15 minutes of the Literacy Hour. The whole class, or a specified group, can do the external activity described in the development section.

Preparation

Collect a few openings to stories that present strongly contrastive settings. A good trio might include a piece of futuristic science fiction (anything by Isaac Asimov), a contemporary domestic story (anything by Anne Fine), and a historical drama (anything by Rosemary Sutcliffe). Optionally, you could also record snippets of video from television programmes or films depicting a similar variety. These clips should be no more than a minute or so long, and should not include any actual narrative. Make copies of photocopiable page 104 for those children carrying out the follow-up work.

Resources needed

Photocopiable page 104, extracts from fiction as specified in 'Preparation', video clips and video recorder (optional), paper, scrap paper, writing materials.

What to do

Introduction

Tell the children that they are going to be exploring the idea of settings in fiction and ask them what they understand by the term 'settings'. If the children are unsure

about it, do not labour at a definition, as their understanding of the term should be developed through the activity itself.

Show the children the three video clips, or read the three extracts to them. After each one ask them what kind of story is likely to follow, what sorts of people are the main characters likely to be and what events are likely to occur. Ask the children to justify their responses with reference to previous reading, listening or viewing. Then ask the children if they can think of any possible developments which are very different from these initial expectations. Offer some possibilities yourself if the children need prompting. (For example, if the setting is contemporary–domestic, such as a supermarket or a disco, you could ask the children to imagine the arrival of a medieval alchemist or a space-station astronaut, and to speculate on how this would affect the atmosphere and likely course of the story.) Summarize this phase of the session by asking the children if they know any stories in which such incongruities occur, and what the author is trying to do by using them.

Development

At this stage the whole class can carry out the development work or you may prefer to work with a selected group while the rest of the class engage in other Literacy Hour activities.

Give the children you are working with just the titles of the two extracts on photocopiable page 104 and ask them to write down or discuss what kind of setting they think is implied by each title. Then distribute copies of photocopiable page 104 and ask them to read the actual settings. This can be done silently or as shared or paired reading. Afterwards, encourage the children to compare their expectations with the actual text. This should reinforce the idea that authors often seek to undermine reader's expectations.

Now ask the children to write a brief outline of how they think the story will develop from the setting. This should be in note form, outlining characters, predicament and resolution. This is best done in groups of three or four in 'brainstorming' fashion, ideas being jotted down on scrap paper. It should not take longer than ten minutes. Allow the groups to share their ideas, then challenge them to write an alternative story plan in which the expectations aroused by the setting are subverted.

Conclusion

The writers can lead a plenary in which they read the settings to the class and ask them to predict what kind of story is likely to emerge. They can then take turns reading out their 'conventional' outlines, followed by their attempts at breaking the conventions.

Finally, you might like to discuss with the class how this type of expectation breaking can lose its power of surprise if it is overdone.

Suggestion(s) for extension

The outlines created by the writing group can be used as blueprints for storywriting, by the group themselves or by anybody in the class. The process of predicting a story from its setting can be incorporated into the discussions you have at storytime and during one-to-one reading. (As one-to-one reading is increasingly conducted only by teaching assistants, you might want to familiarize assistants with the process by asking them to conduct the group work for this activity.)

Suggestion(s) for support

Photocopiable page 104 can be presented as a shared reading activity, and the text can be supported by pictures featuring the scenes and the objects within them. The story outlines can be composed through shared writing. Alternatively, children can be given a simple writing framework with spaces for drawings and notes on characters and plot.

Assessment opportunities

Note the children's ability to make predictions based on prior knowledge. as well as their understanding of notions such as predicament and resolution. You could also assess their critical awareness of the strategies that authors use in order to maintain the reader's attention.

Display ideas

The settings presented on photocopiable page 104 can be illustrated and displayed together with the story plans and any completed stories that emerge from them.

Other aspects of the English PoS covered

Speaking and listening: 1a, b, c, d; 2a, b; 3a, b.
Writing: 1a, b; 2a; 3a.

Reference to photocopiable sheet

Photocopiable page 104 describes two settings. Using firstly just the titles of the passages, the children try to work out what kind of setting is implied. They then write down how they think the story will develop.

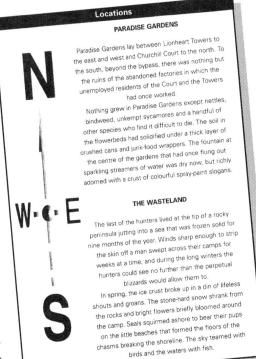

CHARACTER ORIGINS

To familiarize children with the literary or historical origins of characters whose names have entered popular culture. To motivate readers to use information sources in order to extend their knowledge of the origins of popular references.

†† *Class introduction followed by open-ended follow-up.*

⏰ *30 minutes.*

Key background information

There are a great number of names which are used in everyday conversation which originated in fiction or history or both. Frequently, the origins of the characters are known only hazily, if at all, by the people who refer to them. This is a tribute to the vividness and enduring relevance of such characters. This activity is intended to motivate young readers to broaden their reading range by inviting them to do some detective work on the origins of a variety of such names (see below).

Preparation

Working with one or two friends or colleagues, brainstorm a list of character names that most people seem to know. Try to generate about 20 names. Go through your list and ask yourselves whether or not each item refers to a real or fictional character. Do you know who invented the fictional characters, or when the historical ones lived? How much do you know about the character? In what contexts do people refer to the characters in everyday conversation? Are these usages congruent with what you know of the character? How would you go about alleviating your uncertainties about this questions?

Resources needed

A list of well-known names from fiction and/or history, for example: Achilles; Ben Hur; Boadicea; Bonnie and Clyde; Cleopatra; Confucius; Davy Crockett; Doctor Doolittle; Doctor Jekyll; Don Quixote; Dracula; Florence Nightingale; Frankenstein; Hercules; Hiawatha; Houdini; Huckleberry Finn; Jonah; King Canute; Lady Macbeth; Lancelot; Long John Silver; Moby Dick; Oliver Twist; Peter Pan; Pollyanna; Rip Van Winkle; Rob Roy; Robinson Crusoe; Sherlock Holmes; Sinbad the Sailor; Sweeney Todd; Tam O'Shanter; Tarzan; The Queen of Sheba; William Tell. A large-scale matrix of the type presented in the diagram. All these names should be written in the column 'Name'.

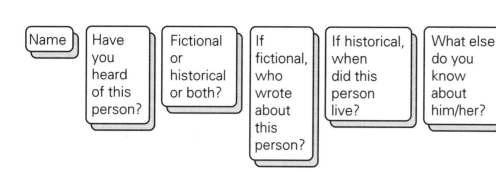

What to do

Introduction

Ask the children to brainstorm a list of names of fictional characters that they have read or heard about. Write down the names, and ask the children to say a few words about each of them. Then ask the class to think of names that they think everybody has heard of. Present your list of names written in the left-hand column of the matrix, and ascertain which are familiar to the children. Conduct a discussion based on the questions in the chart. For example, *Who talks about this person? What do they say? Where might you find out more?*

Development

The initial discussion will probably produce some 'No' responses in the second column, and many other cells will also be left blank. Talk to the children about how they might find out about the unknown characters, or further details about the characters of whom they have heard. This might include searching for the names on the Internet, consulting encyclopaedias, literary companions and dictionaries of mythology and folklore, or simply going and asking somebody about a character's name. Assign an unknown name or an unknown piece of information to each child and ask them to find out as much as they can. It is probably best if this is done informally at the children's initiative.

Conclusion

Put the matrix on display so that you can refer back to it as the information is gathered. For the fictional characters, help children to locate the texts in which they appear, and encourage the class or, depending on interest level, individuals within the class to read those texts. It might be more appropriate for children to read secondary sources; for example, adaptations of 'Macbeth' and *Moby Dick* for younger readers. Urge the children to think about why some historical figures have acquired fictional status, and why some fictional characters (for example Sherlock Holmes) are believed or desired by some people to have been real.

Suggestion(s) for extension

Fluent readers can extend their investigative work to refine answers to the questions already posed. Why do some characters seem to hover between being fictional and non-fictional? What can you find out about the real people underlying some fictional characters (for example Dracula, Robinson Crusoe)? Why are so many of the enduring characters male? What is the balance of heroes to villains? What are the qualities that enable characters to endure? Enduring characters are, by definition, the fruit of past generations; which characters created by contemporary writers are likely to endure?

Suggestion(s) for support

Inexperienced readers can be introduced to analogies based on enduring characters and asked to interpret them. For example, what would you be saying about somebody if you described them as being 'a real Robin Hood', or 'a bit of a Desperate Dan', or 'a Jekyll and Hyde character'? Some of these analogies should be fairly obvious in order to establish the basic idea; some, like the third one above, should be more challenging, requiring further inquiry.

Assessment opportunities

This activity should provide some evidence of the children's previous reading and general knowledge about literary characters. The research element might enable you to assess a child's degree of initiative in using information sources.

Opportunities for IT

The nature of this activity as suggested in 'What to do' lends itself to research. The children could start by searching on electronic encyclopaedias for information about their characters. This could then be extended to looking on the Internet for further information.

Display ideas

Character cards with brief biographies, like those used in the previous activity, can be put on display. The use of moveable cards will enable the children to group the characters according to different criteria (for example, by gender; national origin; into a timeline; into fictional, historical and semi-fictional groups.)

Other aspects of the English PoS covered

Speaking and listening: 1a, b, c, d; 2a, b; 3a, b.
Writing: 1a, b; 2a; 3a.

COMMON PLIGHTS

To familiarize children with some common underlying patterns in story structure: predicament, development and resolution.

†† *Whole class discussion then groups.*

🕑 *20 minutes.*

Key background information

It has often been claimed that all of the stories ever told are based on a handful of common themes. While this might be an exaggeration, it is certainly true that common themes such as virtue rewarded, the biter bit, the overcoming of obstacles and the quest, unite stories that occur in many ages and cultures. These themes probably arise from the universal predicaments or plights that people all over the world encounter in their lives. These plights initiate the complications that trigger off stories and lead eventually to resolutions. This short discussion activity is intended to raise children's awareness of these underlying themes.

This is a discussion activity which need not be confined to the Literacy Hour. It would make a good circle or storytime discussion activity which could later feed into a writers' workshop session.

Preparation

Read through the story frames on photocopiable page 105. The likely development of each story will be obvious to you, but try to visualize a development which would undermine these expectations.

Resources needed

Photocopiable page 105, paper, writing materials.

What to do

Introduction

Explain to the children that you will be reading out some summarized story starts and settings, and that they have to guess what is going to come next. Read out the passages and ask the children for their predictions. In some instances, there might well be complete unanimity in the responses. Ask the children why so many of them are so sure of what is likely to happen. Ask them if they know of any stories which are similar to the outlines, and how they think that the stories implied by the outlines might be resolved.

Development

Read the children one or two models of developments and resolutions that undermine the expectations established by the opening outlines. (For example, all of the king's daughters obey him, and are rewarded handsomely when he returns; Lee is the first man to be eliminated by the invaders.) Get the children to think about why these alternatives sound so unconventional.

Assign story outlines from the photocopiable sheets to groups of children and ask them to compose conventional and unconventional developments and resolutions. This should be done in outline form rather than as full narratives.

Conclusion

Ask the groups to read out their compositions. Conclude by asking the children to think about where the similarities in story pattern come from. (Refer back to the 'Key background information' about universal predicaments if the children need some help.) Point out to them that many traditional stories such as 'Cinderella' and 'St George and the Dragon' have counterparts in many parts of the world.

Suggestion(s) for extension

Story outlines can be written up as full narratives. Fluent readers can be encouraged to identify themes in their everyday fiction reading and to relate them to archetypal patterns – for example, many wilderness adventure stories, such as *Hatchet* by Gary Paulsen (Macmillan), can be related to the archetypal theme of the sojourn in the wilderness; many stories about bullying, such as *Bullies Don't Hurt* by Anthony Masters (Puffin), can be related to the dragon-slaying theme.

Suggestion(s) for support

As a simple way in to this task, inexperienced readers can be helped to keep a diary of reflections on the stories that they read. This can include the frame sentence *This story reminds me of _____*. The children can then relate this to either real-life experience and/or other stories read, heard or viewed.

Assessment opportunities

This activity should give you some idea of the children's previous reading experience, their awareness of underlying structural elements in narrative, and their ability to use these elements creatively in their own writing.

Display ideas

Extracts and illustrations from stories sharing structural elements can be displayed alongside the children's own written and illustrated responses to this activity.

Other aspects of the English PoS covered

Speaking and listening: 1a, b, c, d; 2a, b; 3a, b.
Writing: 1a, b, c; 2a; 3a.

Reference to photocopiable sheet

Photocopiable page 105 provides a number of story starters. Using these, the children must try to identify common patterns and themes.

A LITERATURE TIMELINE

To raise children's awareness of the historical placing of stories and authors, and to encourage them to read fiction from a wider range of historical authors.

†† *Small group initially, preferably quite confident readers, who can then present to the rest of the class.*

🕐 *30 minutes.*

Key background information

The vast majority of the books that are read by children today are produced by contemporary authors. There is nothing surprising or particularly regrettable about this. Publishing for children has expanded massively in the last 30 years or so, and it has often been argued that children's literature did not exist as a distinct field until quite recently. Certainly, some works of fiction which in adapted form have come to be regarded as suitable for children (for example *Oliver Twist*, *Robinson Crusoe*, *Moby Dick*) were never intended for young audiences. However, there are many works of fiction written in earlier decades that children might miss unless they are actively encouraged to seek them out. This is a simple activity aimed at raising children's awareness of earlier literature, and helping them to seek it out.

This activity is an extended, open-ended project and does not fit into the Literacy Hour. Discussion of past authors' work during the Literacy Hour could, however, help to focus children's attention on it.

Preparation

Make a list of some of the earlier published children's books that you have read and find out when they were first published. Mark these dates on a timeline. Make a collection of children's books covering as wide a span of time as you can manage, and put them on display in your classroom. An historical guide to children's literature, such as Robert Leeson's *Reading and Righting* (Collins) or Peter Hunt's *History of Children's Literature* (OUP) should be of help here. A highly entertaining sourcebook for discovering more about historical children's fiction is *The Oxford Treasury of Children's Stories* (OUP) edited by Jan Mark.

Resources needed

A timeline marked off in decades for the 20th century, with a judicious amount of space for earlier centuries (you will probably not be marking much before 1865, the publication date of *Alice in Wonderland*). A collection of old and contemporary books for children (for example, the most recent *Goosebumps* title, a Roald Dahl, an early Enid Blyton, Stevenson's *Treasure Island*, Carroll's *Alice in Wonderland*), encyclopaedias, access to the Internet (if possible).

What to do

Introduction

Give the children time to browse through the display, then prompt them to talk about their reading preferences. Share your own reading experiences and show them the timeline. Ask them to identify the earliest children's books that they know and to estimate whereabouts on the timeline they think they belong. Draw the children's attention to the fact that the books are from a wide timespan and ask them to guess at their places on the timeline. Help the children to check their guesses by referring to the bibliographic information in the book or, if this is incomplete, to information sources such as encyclopaedias or the Internet.

Development

Set the children the challenge of reading from a wider historical range of authors. This will obviously be a long-term project. As the children read, they can record authors and titles on the timeline and add brief reviews to an adjacent display. It is important to avoid coercion – the children should be urged to widen their range, but not forced to persevere with books that they cannot enjoy. Negotiate how you will record the following items:

▲ myths and legends from ancient sources
▲ retellings of folk-tales
▲ modern abridgements and adaptations of classic stories, including those based on Shakespeare plays.

Conclusion

After the group has been working on this project for a few weeks, ask them to share their experiences with the rest of the class in a question and answer session, perhaps recommending particular authors and titles, and summarizing whatever similarities and differences they have found between contemporary and less recent children's literature. The project can then be extended to the rest of the class.

Suggestion(s) for extension

The project provides opportunities for a wide range of in-depth extensions. Children can investigate how common themes in children's literature have changed over the decades; developments in the way that issues such as gender and class are treated (the Narnia stories are a good starting point for this); and more technical points like differences in vocabulary and layout. Children can also investigate the lives and works of favourite authors.

Suggestion(s) for support

Ask less experienced readers to think about when and by whom the books they read were produced (who wrote them). An accessible way into this area is to present children with reading scheme material from the 1950s, 1960s and 1970s, asking them to note the differences in the people and environments that are depicted. (The Janet and John and early Breakthrough readers are a good source for this, and may still be recoverable from the depths of the stockroom.)

Assessment opportunities

The project should provide evidence of readers' motivation, flexibility and curiosity about literature.

Opportunities for IT

This activity lends itself particularly well to research using the Internet. Children can search out the lives of favourite authors and also look for other people's comments and reviews regarding the book they are researching.

Display ideas

The children can display the timeline and reviews in the classroom for other children to read.

Other aspects of the English PoS covered

Speaking and listening: 1a, b, c, d; 2a, b; 3a, b.
Writing: 1a, b, c; 2a; 3a.

A LITERATURE MAP

To familiarize children with literature from a wide range of cultures and to encourage them to read more widely.

†† *Small group initially, preferably quite confident readers, who can then present to the rest of the class.*

⊕ *30 minutes initially, then open-ended follow-up.*

Previous skills/knowledge needed
It will be useful if the children had carried out the previous activity 'A literature timeline' on page 43.

Key background information
Recent years have seen much progress towards the internationalization of the literature that children read, both in the settings of stories and in the range of different nationalities of authors that are read. This is a simple project to raise children's awareness of both of these dimensions.

Preparation
Collect a range of fiction appropriate for the age of the children you teach and from as wide a range of international settings and authorships as you can manage. *The Books for Keeps Guide to Children's Books for a Multicultural Society* would make a good source of information in this respect. Write a few recommendations for books yourself as a guide for the children.

Resources needed
Range of books, as described in 'Preparation', a large world map with coded flags or pins, some written reviews or examples of reviews for the children.

What to do
Introduction
Give the children plenty of time to browse through the display, then ask them to discuss their own recent reading in terms of the range of settings and authors that they have experienced. Devise a code with the children for marking the world map. One method would be to use numbered pins. These could be placed in particular locations and refer to corresponding cards giving bibliographical details and brief reviews of books set in the area marked by the pin or written by an author from that location (you could use different colours for authors and locations).

Development
Over a few weeks, ask the children to concentrate on widening the geographical range of their reading, recording

their experiences on the map and accompanying review cards. Your own recommendations should provide an initial catalyst, and the group should be shown how to use critical guides like *Books for Keeps* magazine, children's literature reviews from *The Guardian* and *The Times Educational Supplement*, and appropriate Internet sites. As with the previous activity, there should be no coercion. The emphasis should be on joint exploration of unfamiliar territory and the sharing of interesting finds.

Conclusion
After a couple of weeks, help the group to present their findings to the rest of the class, who can then be asked to share their own reading experiences and be shown how to record these on the map.

Suggestion(s) for extension
Readers can be helped to compare and contrast themes and styles of children's literature from different countries (looking at differences in dialogue is a good starting point for this). They can also be encouraged to read and review the work of particular authors, and to think about the different levels of availability of literature from various areas (for example, while there are quite a lot of American authors available for English readers, and an increasing number from Australia and New Zealand, there are relatively few from English-speaking Africa.)

Suggestion(s) for support
Make it a habit to talk about the geographical settings and the nationality of the authors of books encountered in one to one, shared and guided reading so that the children gradually become familiar with these aspects of the texts that they encounter.

Assessment opportunities
The project should provide evidence of readers' motivation, flexibility and curiosity about literature.

Opportunities for IT
This activity, as with the previous one, would give the children excellent opportunities to develop research skills using the Internet.

Display ideas
This activity is based around the creation of a display.

Other aspects of the English PoS covered
Speaking and listening: 1a, b, c, d; 2a, b; 3a, b.
Writing: 1a, b, c; 2a; 3a.

Non-fiction

The purposes of the activities in this chapter are to enable readers to become more aware of the ways in which non-fiction text is organized, and to enhance critical appreciation of the information books that they read. As with *Curriculum Bank Reading, Key Stage Two*, many of the activities build upon the pioneering work on Directed Activities Related to Texts (DARTs) by Lunzer and Gardner (Learning from the *Written Word*, Oliver and Boyd).

Readers are encouraged to reflect upon their current knowledge or beliefs about various topics, before generating questions directed at themselves, each other and the text. Co-operative reading and discussion are essential, and specific ideas are provided for helping children to organize their own discussion activities. A range of responses to the information gained from various sources is encouraged. Personal involvement in non-fiction reading is encouraged through activities which prompt the children to offer evaluative and aesthetic responses to their reading.

As with Chapter One, shared reading of sample texts might be fitted into the first part of the Literacy Hour, with focused activities for group and individual work, and some ideas for longer-term open-ended projects.

GENRES WITHIN NON-FICTION

To appreciate that within non-fiction, authors use different language patterns in order to convey different types of information. To identify distinctive features of these genres, including tense. To scan text samples for technical terms and investigate key vocabulary, using dictionaries to check hypotheses based on context and word structure.

†† *Whole-class sharing of text, followed by small-group follow-up.*

🕐 *15–30 minutes for whole-class sharing, 20–40 minutes for follow-up. This can be tailored to correspond to the shared-reading, group-work phases of the Literacy Hour. Depending upon available time and the reading level of the children, this time might be spread over two days, one for each of the genres explored.*

Key background information
Non-fiction conveys information by using a variety of genres which frequently mingle and overlap. For example, recounts are used to retell events and are written in the past tense, using temporal connectives. (***On** the evening of November 5th, 1605, Guy Fawkes entered his hiding place in the cellars of the Houses of Parliament. **After***

checking that he had not been followed...) Explanation genres are used to explain processes or how things work; they are written in the present tense and use causal or temporal connectives. (***In order** to slow the reaction down, graphite rods are lowered into the core...*) These genres frequently alternate as writers shift from descriptions of general processes to accounts of specific episodes. They can interpenetrate when writers switch topics in mid-stream to give parenthetical information, such as a brief note about the history of the discovery of a process. By focusing on the distinctive features of these genres, children can be helped to use them flexibly within their own writing.

Preparation
Make an enlarged copy or OHT reproduction of photocopiable page 106. Also make copies of photocopiable page 106 for each pair of children. Familiarize yourself with further details of the Chernobyl explosion if you do not feel confident about dealing with likely questions on the matter. A schematic diagram of a chain reaction and/or a nuclear reactor would be useful. Decide on a topic of your own that you will discuss with the class during the Introduction.

Resources needed
Photocopiable page 106, board/flip chart, OHP (optional), schematic diagram of a chain reaction and/or nuclear reactor (optional), dictionaries, different-colour marker pens.

What to do

Introduction

Broach the topic of the text that you have decided upon with the class, preferably using reference to some contemporary event that involves similar issues. For example, should we risk importing beef from cows that have been 'grown' by giving them large doses of hormones? Is it justifiable for activists to destroy genetically-modified crops?

Ascertain what the children know already, writing the points that they make on the board or flip chart. Ask the children if they have any questions about this contemporary event and write these as well, prompting the children to bear these in mind as the reading takes place.

Present your enlarged copy (or OHT) of photocopiable page 106 and read it to the children before conducting a shared reading. After this has been done, encourage the children to talk to each other briefly about the gist of the text, before inviting individuals to share their interpretations and their uncertainties with you. In your responses to these, try to relate the children's contributions to their previous knowledge and to their pre-reading questions. Display the diagram of a chain reaction and/or a nuclear reactor if you have created one to provide further explanation.

This discussion will probably lead naturally to the next step: to scan the text for items of vocabulary which are new or whose meanings are unknown or uncertain. Talk these through with the children, demonstrating whenever possible how they can use context or morphology (word structure) to make tentative hypotheses about word meanings. For example, if you were considering context, then in the sentence 'Lethal radiation is what kind of radiation?' you would look at the word 'lethal'. If you were considering morphology then you would analyse the prefix and stem in a word such as 'sub-atomic'. Check the children's hypotheses in a dictionary, demonstrating how to use this tool (opening the book at approximately the right place, using guide words, browsing the columns, interpreting definitions). Question the children in order to encourage them to help you to do this. (*Am I on the right page? Do I turn forward or backward? How do you know?*) Finally, ask the children to share with each other their own revised interpretations of the text.

If time allows, repeat the same process with part two of the text (recount genre). Alternatively, this can be done on a different day.

Development (whole class or focused group)

Provide pairs of children with photocopies of the Chernobyl text. Ask the children to re-read it, noting the descriptive features of the first text and the storylike (narrative) features of the second. Draw particular attention to differences in verb tenses and connectives. These features can be highlighted using different colour marker pens.

For vocabulary extension work, ask the children to highlight technical vocabulary and to write their own definitions based on the whole-class discussion.

Conclusion

If a group has been doing this work, they can share their findings with the whole class and the class can be asked to predict what happened next. You could also ask them what might have happened if things had turned out differently. Children could be asked to find out more about this or similar episodes in their own time and share their discoveries with the class on another day.

Suggestion(s) for extension

The alternation between explanatory and recount genres is a very common feature of non-fiction, and competent readers can be encouraged to seek out examples related to their own interests. These can be used as models for their own writing. Examples might include:

▲ Explanation of iceberg formation/recount of the sinking of the Titanic.

▲ Explanation of aerodynamics of flight/recount of the first flight by man.

▲ Explanation of how fires can start spontaneously/recount about how early humans might first have discovered fire.

Suggestion(s) for support

Less accomplished readers can follow 'Suggestion(s) for extension' above but can be helped to read and to compose briefer alternating genre texts in which the subject matter is closer to immediate experience and hence uses more familiar vocabulary. For example:

If you leave stuff like bread uncovered in a warm damp place, it gets covered in mould. Mould is a type of fungus. It produces millions of spores that drift about in the air until they land in a place that will allow them to grow into new moulds.

One day, a researcher called Alexander Fleming...

Assessment opportunities

Note the children's ability to identify patterns of difference between genres, and to handle these patterns in their own writing. Also note their ability to use context and morphology to estimate word meanings and to check meanings in dictionaries.

Opportunities for IT

Children could research the topics on the photocopiable sheets or the ones they carry out for the extension and support activities using either a CD-ROM or the Internet. Any information they find out could be typed up on the word processor, thus creating their own photocopiable pages.

The word processor is the ideal tool for encouraging pupils to craft their writing in this non-fiction genre, ensuring that tenses are correct, or rewording sections to make them clearer to the reader. The children could also use a word-processed version of the text and use different font colours or other formatting to mark the differences in verb tenses or connectives.

Display ideas

The written work suggested in 'Suggestion(s) for extension and support' can be displayed with captions which highlight the differences in language between the genre features used.

Other aspects of the English PoS covered

Speaking and listening: 1a; 2a, b.
Writing: 1a, b, c; 2a, b, c, d, e; 3a, b, c.

Reference to photocopiable sheet

Photocopiable page 106 is an information text about nuclear explosions and nuclear reactors. It also gives a recount of the incidents on the night of the Chernobyl explosion. The children consider both texts and the way in which language can differ within non-fiction writing.

Episode at Chernobyl

Nuclear explosions are the most destructive events ever to have occurred on Earth. They are caused by a process called nuclear fission, which occurs when the nucleus of an atom of a radioactive substance such as uranium or plutonium splits. The nucleus can be made to split by bombarding it with sub-atomic particles known as neutrons. The splitting of the atom releases a massive amount of heat energy and more neutrons, which strike neighbouring atoms, causing them to split as well, releasing yet more energy and yet more neutrons. This is known as a nuclear chain reaction, an immensely powerful process which is very difficult to control.

In an atom bomb, the chain reaction takes place in a fraction of a second, causing a vast explosion and the release of lethal radiation. In a nuclear reactor, rods of uranium or plutonium are lowered into a reactor which causes a slower chain reaction to begin. The reaction generates a huge amount of heat which is used to create steam for the generation of electricity. The speed of the reaction can be controlled by inserting into the reactor rods of a substance such as graphite, which absorbs the escaping neutrons. Lowering the control rods completely can shut the reactor down. When the control rods are lifted, the reaction speeds up. To prevent the escape of radiation, the reactor is encased in a steel shell surrounded by concrete.

During the night of Friday 24th – Saturday 25th April, 1986, a team of engineers were preparing Reactor 4 at the Chernobyl nuclear power station in the Ukraine for shutdown. This would enable them to carry out maintenance and repairs. They also hoped that when the flow of energy had decreased to a certain point, they would be able to carry out some important tests before shutdown. Graphite control rods were inserted into the reactor core, and the flow of energy began to slow down. At about midnight, the engineers attempted to begin the tests, but they discovered that the power of the reactor was already too low. The two head engineers judged that it was now too late for the tests to take place, and that the reactor should be allowed to shut down. Their supervisor, however, was impatient for the tests to go ahead, and decided to risk a rapid restart of the reactor. He ordered that the control rods should be immediately raised.

The engineers obeyed, and a huge blast of energy surged through the system, straining the pipes and turbines which processed the steam. By 1.23am the whole system appeared to be at breaking point, and one of the engineers announced that he was going to press an emergency button that would lower all the control rods into the reactor. Had he succeeded, the power station might have been saved. But the rods jammed, and seconds later there was a vast explosion.

FORMALITY AND AUTHORITY

To enable children to identify formal and informal aspects of the language of report writing. To compare formal and informal reports, discussing and assessing their reliability. To talk about the sources of information used by writers of purported non-fiction. To develop critical awareness of the author's perception of readership.

✝✝ *Whole-class shared reading and discussion. The coding of 'facts' can be done as a whole class or as a guided-group or independent activity.*

🕐 *15–30 minutes for each text type, spread over two days if necessary.*

Key background information

It is often assumed that information texts should be written in a neutral, impersonal, objective manner. This type of writing can be challenging for some children who prefer texts to be humorous and personally engaging. Writers of non-fiction have often attempted to incorporate humour and informality into their work, but this has been criticized by strict adherents to genre theory, who argue that children should be taught to deal with the characteristics of authentic texts. Formality is closely tied to the idea of authority: a text written in a formal manner can give the impression of being more reliable than one which is written in a more personal register. However, the reliability of an information text is, of course, based upon the verifiability of the information it conveys rather than the style in which it is written. This activity provides a playful opportunity for children to discuss these issues. Two pairs of texts are provided. One pair is factual but informal; the other formal but fictitious.

Preparation

Prepare enlarged copies of photocopiable pages 107 and 108. Read up on the subject matter of the factual texts if necessary (the elephant's trunk and the tardigrade). The elephant and rat louse texts are more challenging than the tardigrade and bibliogar. Collect examples of texts which illustrate differences between formal and informal approaches to information (for example tabloid and quality newspapers, popular and academic science books).

Resources needed

Photocopiable pages 107–108, the text samples specified in 'Preparation', board/flip chart, paper, writing materials, dictionary.

What to do

Introduction

Familiarize the children with the issues mentioned above by reading to them from the formal and informal texts that you have gathered together. Ask them to identify the features which make a text appear to be formal or informal; using the terms 'friendly' and 'unfriendly' might be an effective way of introducing this distinction. Also ask the children where they think writers of information texts get their information from. Is a writer of books about wildlife necessarily writing from personal experience? If not, where has the author got his or her 'facts' from, and how reliable are they?

Ask the children what different writing styles imply about the author's perception of his or her audience. You could introduce this point by asking the children who the author thought that he or she was writing for. *What age group did he or she have in mind? How well informed did the author consider the reader to be? How does the author attempt to inform and entertain the reader?*

Development

Conduct a shared reading of photocopiable page 107 (informal/factual). This can be either the elephant's trunk text or the tardigrade text. Ask the children whether or not this is a formally written text, and highlight the features on which the children's decisions are based. For example, direct address to the reader; use of the first person; attempted humour; use of exclamation marks.

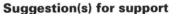

Identify any unfamiliar vocabulary and ask the children to make hypotheses about the word meanings based on context and word structure. Check the word meanings in a dictionary, then ask the children to discuss the text in pairs in order to identify all the new information that it has provided. Allow five to ten minutes for this, then ask each pair of children to contribute one fact while you write them up on the board or flip chart.

Repeat this procedure with text two from photocopiable page 108 (formal/fictitious). This can be either the rat louse or the bibliogar text. At this stage, do not tell the children that this text is a spoof, but deal frankly with any doubts raised by the children as to the authenticity of the information. When this has been done, distribute paper and writing materials to the children and present the two 'fact' lists written on the board. Ask the children to grade them according to the following code:

1. I knew this already.
2. This is new information, but I believe it.
3. This is new information, and I would want to have it checked.
4. I don't believe this.

Ask the children to compare their lists in pairs or small groups. For 'facts' of type two and three, ask them to suggest what sources they would need to verify the author's claims. For type four statements, ask the children

to speculate about why the author might be making doubtful statements. In this respect, it is important to note that the elephants' trunks text is based upon a passage in *The Language Instinct* by Stephen Pinker (Penguin) and that one of Pinker's sources was the poem 'Sacred Elephant' by Heathcote Williams, a polemic against the hunting of elephants. The tardigrade text is based on an article in *Nature* as reported by *The Guardian*. This might lead into a discussion of how the press 'cherry picks' exotic information from scientific sources, possibly distorting it in the process. The authors' imagination represented in the spoof texts might also be discussed.

Conclusion

Finally, summarize the characteristics of formal and informal texts, writing them up if you like. Encourage the children to apply this knowledge to their everyday reading of information texts and media such as newspapers, magazines and broadcasts.

Suggestion(s) for extension

Children can conduct investigations into a range of texts on a specific topic, discussing aspects of writing style and assessing them for reliability. Inconsistencies between texts effectively stimulate this type of discussion, and collections of old history and geography text books, or newspapers from different ends of the political spectrum, are invaluable sources of such inconsistencies.

Suggestion(s) for support

This activity can be carried out purely orally, with an enlarged text on display. When the facts are coded, you or an assistant can help children to locate them in the text, using different-coloured pens to highlight them according to whether they believe them, are doubtful or totally disbelieve them. The 'What to do' section can also be carried out with less demanding texts, including extracts from newspapers and popular magazines.

Assessment opportunities

Note the children's knowledge of features such as direct address, use of first person and punctuation conventions. Note also their critical awareness of the author's perception of audience and the reliability of sources.

Opportunities for IT

The children could extend this activity by using the Internet to research information from a variety of sources and then compare the information they find. Common themes and topics such as the water cycle or Ancient Greeks will provide a range of different information texts to use. This should lead to discussions about the validity of information on the Internet.

Display ideas

Extracts from texts from a range of sources on a specific subject can be displayed, the statements in them highlighted according to the code outlined in 'What to do'.

Other aspects of the English PoS covered

Speaking and listening: 1a, b, c; 2a, b; 3a, b.

Reference to photocopiable sheets

Photocopiable pages 107–108 give information about various animals and insects. However, the two extracts on photocopiable page 108 are fictitious even though they are written in a more authoritative tone. The children analyse the texts and discuss the characteristics of formal and informal texts.

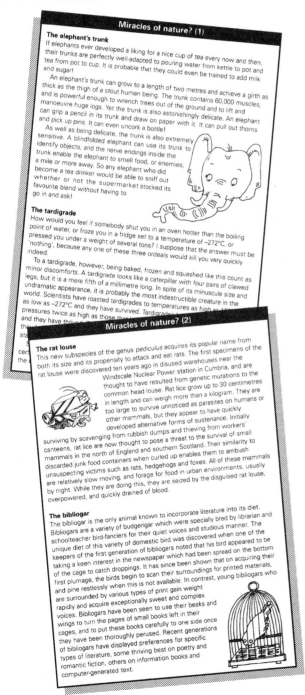

Miracles of nature? (1)

The elephant's trunk

If elephants ever developed a liking for a nice cup of tea every now and then, their trunks are perfectly well-adapted to pouring water from kettle to pot and tea from pot to cup. It is probable that they could even be trained to add milk and sugar!

An elephant's trunk can grow to a length of two metres and achieve a girth as thick as the thigh of a stout human being. The trunk contains 60,000 muscles, and is powerful enough to wrench trees out of the ground and to lift and manoeuvre huge logs. Yet the trunk is also astonishingly delicate. An elephant can grip a pencil in its trunk and draw on paper with it. It can pull out thorns and pick up pins. It can even uncork a bottle!

As well as being delicate, the trunk is also extremely sensitive. A blindfolded elephant can use its trunk to identify objects, and the nerve endings inside the trunk enable the elephant to smell food, or enemies, a mile or more away. So any elephant who did become a tea drinker would be able to sniff out whether or not the supermarket stocked its favourite blend without having to go in and ask!

The tardigrade

How would you feel if somebody shut you in an oven hotter than the boiling point of water, or froze you in a fridge set to a temperature of –272°C, or pressed you under a weight of several tons? I suppose that the answer must be 'nothing', because any one of these three ordeals would kill you very quickly indeed.

To a tardigrade, however, being baked, frozen and squashed like this count as minor discomforts. A tardigrade looks like a caterpillar with four pairs of clawed legs, but it is a mere fifth of a millimetre long. In spite of its minuscule size and undramatic appearance, it is probably the most indestructible creature in the world. Scientists have roasted tardigrades to temperatures as high as [...], as low as –272°C and they have survived. Tardigrades [...] pressures twice as high as those that [...] and they have thriv[...]

Miracles of nature? (2)

The rat louse

This new subspecies of the genus *pediculus* acquires its popular name from both its size and its propensity to attack and eat rats. The first specimens of the rat louse were discovered ten years ago in disused warehouses near the Windscale Nuclear Power station in Cumbria, and are thought to have resulted from genetic mutations to the common head louse. Rat lice grow up to 30 centimetres in length and can weigh more than a kilogram. They are too large to survive unnoticed as parasites on humans or other mammals, but they appear to have quickly developed alternative forms of sustenance. Initially surviving by scavenging from rubbish dumps and thieving from workers' canteens, rat lice are now thought to pose a threat to the survival of small mammals in the north of England and southern Scotland. Their similarity to discarded junk food containers when curled up enables them to ambush unsuspecting victims such as rats, hedgehogs and foxes. All of these mammals are relatively slow moving, and forage for food in urban environments, usually by night. While they are doing this, they are seized by the disguised rat louse, overpowered, and quickly drained of blood.

The bibliogar

The bibliogar is the only animal known to incorporate literature into its diet. Bibliogars are a variety of budgerigar which were specially bred by librarian and schoolteacher bird-fanciers for their quiet voices and studious manner. The unique diet of this variety of domestic bird was discovered when one of the keepers of the first generation of bibliogars noted that his bird appeared to be taking a keen interest in the newspaper which had been spread on the bottom of the cage to catch droppings. It has since been shown that on acquiring their first plumage, the birds begin to scan their surroundings for printed materials, and pine restlessly when this is not available. In contrast, young bibliogars who are surrounded by various types of print gain weight rapidly and acquire exceptionally sweet and complex voices. Bibliogars have been seen to use their beaks and wings to turn the pages of small books left in their cages, and to put these books carefully to one side once they have been thoroughly perused. Recent generations of bibliogars have displayed preferences for specific types of literature, some thriving best on poetry and romantic fiction, others on information books and computer-generated text.

BIAS IN INFORMATION TEXTS

To enable children to assess the viewpoints from which 'factual' texts are written.

†† *Whole-class discussion, with an opportunity for small-group follow-up.*

🕐 *30 minutes.*

Key background information

The fact that the information in non-fiction books has been selected by a writer and is presented from that writer's point of view is often neglected. This activity gives children the opportunity to discuss the issue.

Preparation

Read up on the lives of Christopher Columbus and Che Guevara if necessary. Collect news items from different newspapers in which events or personalities are described from contrasting points of view – letters pages and Internet discussion groups are a good source for this. Make an enlarged copy of photocopiable page 109. The Che Guevara texts are more challenging than the Columbus ones. Preceding this lesson, ask the children to find out whatever they can about the two personalities in question, stressing that some people believe them to be heroes, while others believe them to be villains. Talk to the children about their own heroes, and what it is that makes a person into one.

Resources needed

Photocopiable page 109, media material as specified in 'Preparation', board/flip chart. For the extension activity – paper, writing materials.

What to do

Introduction

Before presenting the texts to the class, hold some discussion around the idea of bias. Talking about rival accounts of events, issues and personalities from newspapers representing different political opinions is a good way of stimulating this. Present the media material you have obtained to the class to generate discussion. The behaviour of sporting and entertainment personalities can often give rise to conflicting accounts of events, and children are generally well-informed and eager to discuss this type of thing.

Development

Conduct a class reading of one of the biographies on photocopiable page 109, and afterwards ask the children what perceptions they now have of the person. Help the children to identify the words and phrases that have created this impression, underlining them and explaining them if necessary.

Now conduct a class reading of the second biography

of the person and repeat this process. Make a double list on the board or flip chart, setting out the words and phrases that have been used to describe related events, and grouping them under the headings of 'hero' and 'villain'. Ask the children to speculate on why writers make the choices that they do in this respect. For example, how might a surviving Carib inhabitant have described Columbus' exploits?

Extend the list by bringing in examples such as 'stern disciplinarian' versus 'tyrant'. Continue by putting other examples under the hero and villain headings, and asking the children to suggest the matching term for the other column. This does not have to be a term that actually appears in the text, just one that contradicts the term in the opposite column.

Conclusion
Summarize the main points of the lesson:
▲ The same set of 'facts' can be interpreted either negatively or positively.
▲ Writers do not present facts, but interpretations.
▲ Interpretations are based on the opinions and or interests of the writer.
Encourage the children to look out for bias in other texts. They can bring in any that they find to share with the rest of the class.

Suggestion(s) for extension
Children could do further reading on either or both of the biographies, perhaps attempting to conclude for themselves whether or not the personalities were heroes, villains or a combination of both. Children could also be asked to write entries for imaginary encyclopaedias of the 22nd century, in which today's celebrities are represented either as heroes or villains.

Suggestion(s) for support
Relate the idea of bias to media accounts of the behaviour of contemporary celebrities. Are certain sports people yobs or loveable rascals?

Assessment opportunities
Note the children's awareness of bias, and their ability to

identify the connotations of the author's vocabulary choices.

Opportunities for IT
If the children are given word-processed versions of the texts they could highlight all the villain/hero words and phrases in different colours. These words could then be 'cut and pasted' to make a heroes/villains list underneath the text. If the children use the 'copy' facility, rather than 'cut' they can make a copy of each word underneath the text, leaving the original in place.

Alternatively, once they have highlighted each of the hero/villain words and phrases they could go back to the text and change each one to reverse the picture created, or make their own.

Display ideas
Contrasting accounts of events and personalities can be collected and displayed, with 'loaded' vocabulary highlighted. The children's biographies for a 22nd century encyclopaedia could also be illustrated with pictures of the personalities depicted.

Other aspects of the English PoS covered
Speaking and listening: 1a, b, c; 2a, b; 3b.

Reference to photocopiable sheet
Photocopiable page 109 provides two biographies of Christopher Columbus and Che Guevara. For each figure one biography is positive while the other is critical. The children use these biographies to consider the notion of bias in texts.

Biographies

Guevara, Ernesto 'Che' (1928–67): Argentinian communist and revolutionary. After graduating as a doctor in 1953, Guevara abandoned medicine for politics, and played a key role in the violent overthrow of the Cuban government, helping Fidel Castro to seize power and establish his dictatorship in 1959. He held government posts after the revolution, but in 1965 he left Cuba in order to spread communist doctrine in other impoverished countries. He is known to have attempted to lead an unsuccessful insurrection in central Africa before returning to South America. During an incompetent campaign against the Bolivian government, he led his troops into an ambush. Guevara was captured and executed in October 1967.

Guevara, Che (Ernesto) (1928–67): Argentinian doctor and liberation leader, given the affectionate nickname 'Che' by his admirers. Che graduated in medicine in 1953, but soon afterwards decided that he could best relieve suffering by fighting injustice rather than disease. He played a key role in the heroic struggle that overthrew the Batista dictatorship in Cuba, and afterwards assisted his friend Fidel Castro in the government of the liberated country. In 1965, leading a brave but doomed campaign in central Africa before returning to lead a liberation movement in Bolivia. Che was captured by Bolivian forces in October 1967. In spite of being wounded, he offered to treat enemy casualties, but he was murdered by his captors and his body buried in secret.

Columbus, Christopher (1451–1506): Genoan mariner and explorer, discoverer of the New World. Columbus first went to sea at the age of 14, and survived a shipwreck in 1470. Seven years later he began to seek a patron for a bold expedition to sail westward to India: an idea which was greeted with ridicule and disbelief. Eventually he found backing from Ferdinand and Isabella of Castille, and in 1492 embarked on the journey that was to bring him to the Caribbean and the Americas. Columbus made four voyages to the New World, all of them frought with great danger and he had to cope with difficulties from travelling companions who were less bold than he was. He died in Spain and his remains lie in Seville cathedral.

Colon, Cristobal (1451–1506): Genoan merchant and adventurer who initiated the colonialization of the Caribbean and the Americas and the extermination of their original inhabitants. Colon conceived the idea that India could be reached by sailing west, and after receiving royal backing from Ferdinand and Isabella of Castille, he set off in August 1492 and reached the Caribbean in October. Colon was not a skilled mariner, and this and subsequent voyages were frought with great danger for his crew members, whom he treated very harshly. Colon's establishment of settlements in the New World directly led to the destruction of the civilizations of the original inhabitants.

LISTEN, SUMMARIZE AND QUESTION

To enable children to extract main ideas from information texts. To introduce children to the distinction between open and closed questions.

†† *Whole class.*

🕒 *20–30 minutes.*

Key background information

A distinction is often made between literal and inferential comprehension. The first involves recall of information explicitly stated in the text, the second requires the reader to go beyond the given information by applying background knowledge and critical judgement to this information. These 'levels' of comprehension are related to closed and open questions. This activity involves direct teaching of these distinctions through an oral procedure which reverses the conventional format for comprehension activities. Instead of answering questions on a given text, children are taught how to offer their own questions to the text.

This is a text-sentence-level discussion activity that might fit into the second 15 minutes of the Literacy Hour. Alternatively, it can be based on foundation subject text outside the Literacy Hour.

Preparation

Make an enlarged copy of a non-fiction text related to the interests and ability of your class, ensuring that you have a photocopying licence first. Make sure the title of the text is included. Divide it into four or five chunks which can be presented in sequence. A chunk can consist of a sentence, a paragraph or two or three linked paragraphs, depending on the reading stamina of your pupils. Read the text yourself, and for each chunk compose a brief summary of the main idea or ideas. Also think of one closed question related to the explicit content of the chunk, and one open question relating to unstated assumptions, uncertainties, or issues such as bias and reliability. For the former type of question, there should be an unambiguous answer present in the text itself; for the latter there might be several answers which require reflection on the information in the text.

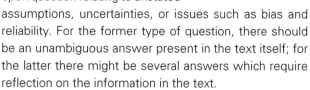

Resources needed

An appropriate text as specified in 'Preparation', related questions, board/flip chart. For the extension activity – writing materials, highlighter pens.

What to do

Introduction

Introduce the children to the terms 'summary' and 'open and closed questions'. You might say that in a summary, the most important information is restated and the rest left out. For a closed question, you can find the answer 'right there' in what has just been read. For an open question, you have to 'think and link', making connections between what is 'right there' and what is already known. Stress that for open questions, there may be several answers.

Development

Show the children the title of the text you have selected and give them a couple of minutes to make predictions based on the title. Then tell them what the text is about and ask them to talk about what they already know about the subject and what they would like to find out.

Conduct a shared reading of the whole text, dealing with any difficulties as they arise. Then return to the first chunk and read it aloud to the children. Then perform a 'think aloud' process, in which you decide upon the most important idea or ideas in each chunk. Talk the children through the selection and rejection process involved in making this decision, and note your ideas down on the board or flip chart. This is really just making audible and visible the steps you went through when you prepared the activity. In a similar way, talk your way through composing a closed question, stressing that the answer must be 'right there' in the text. Repeat the process with an open question, stressing 'think and link'.

Ensure that the children are clear about these three terms (summary, open question, closed question), then read aloud the second chunk, and ask the children to work in pairs and to compose orally a summary, a closed question and an open question related to it. Allow about five minutes for this, then ask the children to offer their ideas. Talk through these responses, and write up the best ones on the same sheet as your models for the first chunk, carefully explaining why you have chosen the ones you have. Repeat this process with the rest of the text.

Conclusion

Read through the collected responses with the children and revise the process you went through in order to produce them. Help the children to compose a brief summary of the text as a whole.

Suggestion(s) for extension

Once this process has been modelled a number of times on texts of different levels of complexity, children who

are more independent can be helped to apply it to the texts that they share during guided reading time. Highlighter pens can be used to identify main ideas and to mark portions of text which stimulate questions. Responses can be written down.

Suggestion(s) for support

Practise this technique with familiar stories. You could start by asking the children for brief summaries of well-known fairytales, or of recent episodes of favourite television programmes. This also provides good material for modelling open and closed questioning. For example:

▲ Closed: Which of the three bears did Goldilocks most upset?

▲ Open: How should Goldilocks recompense the three bears, if at all?

Assessment opportunities

Note the children's ability to distinguish key ideas and peripheral detail. This activity should also provide information about children's ability to recall literal detail and to read beyond the given information.

Opportunities for IT

The children could use a word processor to write and edit their summaries, particularly of well-known stories. A word count, of perhaps 100 or 200 words, could be given so that the children have to craft their summary to fit the allowed word count. This will help them to focus on the key information and also on how sentences can be altered to reduce the words but convey the same meaning.

Alternatively the children could write their own summary passage and prepare one literal and one inferential question for another child to answer.

Display ideas

Summaries and examples of question types can be displayed alongside the texts from which they have been extracted. Colour-coded highlighters can be used to identify the portions of the original text from which the summary and questions have been drawn.

Other aspects of the English PoS covered

Speaking and listening: 1a, b, c, d; 2a, b; 3a, b.
Writing: 1a, b, c; 2a; 3a.

LEXICAL COHESION IN INFORMATION TEXTS

To help children to appreciate the role played by subject-specific vocabulary in establishing the reader's expectations about the nature of a text. To enable children to use expectations about the general nature of a text to arrive at the meanings of difficult words. To practise using a dictionary.

†† *Whole class with small group follow-up.*

🕐 *15 minutes with 20 minutes follow-up.*

Key background information

Every subject area has its own jargon, and some of the difficulties that readers encounter with non-fiction texts arise from interpretation of this vocabulary. Particular problems can arise not just with technical vocabulary that learners may not have met before, but also when words that learners are familiar with in everyday contexts are used with different meanings within a specialized text. This activity gives readers the opportunity to think about such potential difficulties and to practise strategies for dealing with them.

Preparation

Obtain some pictures of pumpkins as stimuli, or some real pumpkins. (Most children find these fascinating.) Read photocopiable page 110 and highlight in different colours technical words and familiar words that have been used with specialized meanings. An example is given for the first passage in 'What to do'. Enlarge photocopiable page 110. Write out the word sets for each passage onto coloured cards, one colour for each category. Select one or two examples of common words that have different meanings (for example *iron* or *rich* from the first passage).

Resources needed

Pumpkins or pictures of pumpkins, photocopiable page 110, cards bearing the words specified above, dictionaries of an appropriate level for the class, plus an adult dictionary. For the extension activity – thesauri.

What to do

Introduction

Show the children the pumpkins or the pictures of them and encourage them to talk about what they already know about pumpkins and what they would like to find out about them. Explain that they are going to be looking at three different passages about pumpkins, each reflecting a different type of interest, and that they will be attempting to guess the occupations or interests of each author.

Development

Show the children the 'technical vocabulary' word sets pertaining to the first passage (see the diagram opposite).

technical vocabulary	familiar words – special meanings
nutritious	flesh
cultivate(d)	rich
vitamin(s)	mineral(s)
digestible	high
carbohydrate	level(s)
protein	sugar(s)
polyunsaturated	fibre
edible	iron
nutrient(s)	fat(s)

Talk about the words in the first set, ascertaining the children's knowledge of them, and demonstrating how to use the dictionary in order to find out more. Next, display the second list (of familiar words) and see how many possible different meanings or connotations the children can come up with for them generally. Talk about possibilities that might not have been mentioned, then turn again to the dictionaries and look up the meanings there. Bear in mind that it is very likely that your class dictionary set may have neither technical vocabulary such as *polyunsaturated*, nor the exact shade of meaning for a word like *iron* when it refers to a trace element. It is a good idea always to have an adult dictionary to hand, but if you have to rely on this you may find that the language of the definitions is beyond the reach of the children. These points are addressed again in the next activity.

After these initial stages, it is likely that the children will be able to guess the relevant profession or interest of the author of the first extract. Conduct a shared reading in order to confirm this, highlighting the words that you have examined, and discussing their meanings in the light of the passage.

Now present the second passage, and ask the children to watch while you read through the text fairly rapidly, stopping at each example of technical vocabulary. Repeat the process of discussing these words, looking them up and then predicting what the particular focus of the passage is before reading it together and examining the words in context.

Conclusion
Present the third passage and ask the children to go through the procedure themselves. Afterwards, discuss the passage and the highlighted words.

Suggestion(s) for extension
Fluent readers can research the semantic fields of various subject areas; that is to say, the vocabulary related to that topic, together with relationships between them such as synonymy and hyponymy. (For example, in the first text, *vitamin, fat, protein, sugar* and *mineral* are hyponyms of *nutrient*.) Target vocabulary can also be categorized into nouns, verbs and adjectives, and the morphology of technical words can be examined (for example, the root shared by *nutritious, nutrient* and words outside the text such as *nourishment* and *malnutrition*). Polysemy, the fact that one word can carry several meanings, is a rich source for further research. Children can be given a word and asked to browse dictionaries and thesauri and to collect as many meanings as they can find, indicating which of these meanings are related and which are not. (For example, the word *port* bears at least half a dozen meanings, some clustered around the concept of carrying, others not.)

Suggestion(s) for support
The word-collecting work advocated in 'Suggestion(s) for extension' should be conducted with struggling readers at a more basic level. It is often a good idea to identify words which are likely to cause difficulty before the reading of a text and to discuss them beforehand, then to discuss them again when they are met with in context. When approaching a new topic, it can be useful to look at its jargon beforehand and to help children to prepare illustrated glossaries. It is important that less able readers are given a lot of support in the use of dictionaries. Definitions on their own will not help the novice to unlock the meaning of a word as it occurs in a particular context.

Assessment opportunities
This activity will provide opportunities to assess learners' current vocabulary level, and their ability to learn new words and derive new meanings for familiar words.

Opportunities for IT

The children could work on a word-processed version of the final text, marking all of the technical vocabulary in a different colour. More able pupils might use different colours to highlight nouns, verbs and adjectives.

These words could be listed underneath the passage, either by typing them again, or by copying and then pasting them from the text. Children could then use a paper or electronic dictionary to look up the meanings of the words. An interesting extension would be to replace the technical words with less technical explanations that retained the meaning of the text. This will underline the importance of technical vocabulary.

Display ideas

Research into semantic fields can be displayed as word webs indicating relationships between roots and the word families that they generate. The illustrated glossaries mentioned in the 'Suggestion(s) for support' can also be displayed as charts.

Other aspects of the English PoS covered

Speaking and listening: 1a, b, c, d; 2a, b; 3a, b.
Writing: 1a, b, c; 2a; 3a.

Reference to photocopiable sheet

Photocopiable page 110 contains three pieces of text referring to pumpkins. Each piece of text is written from a different viewpoint and contains language specific to the different area of interest.

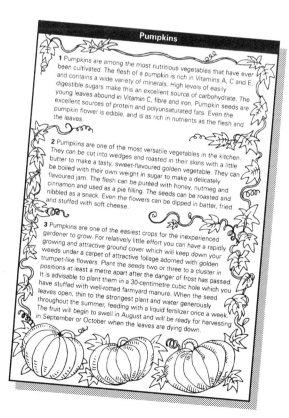

COMPARING DICTIONARIES

To enable children to practise using dictionaries and to become familiar with dictionary conventions. To develop critical awareness of dictionary writing.

†† *Whole-class introduction followed by small-group work.*

🕐 *30 minutes plus open-ended follow-up.*

Key background information

It is often assumed that children can teach themselves to navigate dictionaries once the basics of alphabetical order have been mastered. This is a faulty assumption, since dictionaries have many specific genre features unrelated to alphabetical order, and children require explicit instruction in these features. Furthermore, dictionaries vary in the helpfulness of their language and layout features. Traditional 'definese' is notoriously difficult for children to master. This activity introduces children to dictionary features, engages them in creating their own definitions, and attempts to nurture critical awareness of dictionary quality.

The comparative presentation of dictionaries can be done in the first 15 minutes of the Literacy Hour; more focused work can be done by one or more groups during guided or independent reading.

Preparation

Select two or three dictionaries produced by different publishers, but all aimed at the age-range that you teach. (Oxford, Collins, Chambers and Unwin are all publishers whose material you may have in your classroom.) Prepare a list of four or five words that are relatively new to the class, such as technical vocabulary from a subject area the children are studying, or items of unfamiliar vocabulary that you have come across in a book that you are reading to the class. If you have a photocopying licence, make sufficient photocopies of corresponding pages, carrying definitions of one or two of these words so that there is one for each pair or small group. Assess the helpfulness of the dictionaries in the light of the criteria below.
▲ Clarity of language used.
▲ Style of definition: for example:
define: to explain the meaning of a word (traditional)
define: When you define a word, you provide an explanation of its meaning (transparent).
stubborn: difficult to persuade (traditional)
stubborn: If a person is stubborn, it is difficult to make them change their mind (transparent).
▲ Use of example sentences. (The teacher asked Jenny to define the word 'translucent'.) Note that more recently published dictionaries tend to use transparent definitions, but that example sentences might be provided with either type of definition, or omitted altogether.

▲ Use of diagrams or illustrations.

▲ Layout features: use of guide words; size of font; use of bold, italic and so on, number of words per page.

Resources needed

List of unfamiliar words, dictionaries (there should be enough for one of each type of dictionary between two children), photocopies of relevant pages, paper, writing materials, board/flip chart.

What to do

Introduction

Write the target vocabulary on the board or flip chart and remind the children of the context in which it was introduced. Ask the children to talk to each other about what they think the words mean. After a couple of minutes, ask for volunteers to offer definitions and examples of sentences containing the words to the class. Ask other children to comment on these. With the class, decide on a definition or two, helping the children to refine their wording. Next, distribute the photocopies of the dictionary definitions and point out the features that you have considered in your preparation. Ensure that the children are familiar with features such as guide words, example sentences and different styles of definition. You might also introduce the term 'headword' to identify the item that is being defined. Conduct a shared reading of the published definitions and, using the criteria listed above, lead a discussion comparing critically the dictionary definitions with those composed by the children.

Development

Present the selected group with the full word list and the dictionaries from which you have taken the copies. Remind the group of the stages of activity that you have just demonstrated with the class, and help them to extend the activity to the rest of the words on the list. Set them the target of creating their own definition and example sentence for each word, together with a critical summary of the definitions offered by the dictionaries.

Conclusion

The group can then present their work to the whole class.

Suggestion(s) for extension

Help confident readers and writers to conduct an in-depth analysis of the dictionaries used throughout the school. This can be initiated through the procedures described above, and extended via survey procedures in which they interview children or use questionnaires in order to evaluate children's opinions about dictionaries and the problems that they have with them. They might also write to publishers and lexicographers about the issues involved in compiling dictionaries.

Suggestion(s) for support

This activity can be extended over a longer period, the sessions being judiciously paced and separated, so that children less familiar with dictionaries and definitions can explore one or two words and definitions each day. This activity should be regularly revisited with new words that less able readers come across in their routine reading. It is important that such readers are taught how to use the dictionary through demonstrations during shared or paired reading.

Assessment opportunities

Opportunities should arise in this activity for assessing children's abilities to comprehend and compose definitions, to use new words in context, and to assess resources critically.

Display ideas

Pages from different dictionaries can be photocopied and features such as headwords, guide words, example sentences and additional information can be highlighted, labelled and critically compared. The children can be helped to prepare an enlarged version of a dictionary page of their own which can be displayed alongside the published examples.

Other aspects of the English PoS covered

Speaking and listening: 1a, b, c; 2a, b; 3a, b.
Writing: 1a, b; 2a; 3a.

INFORMATION EXCHANGE

To enable children to extract main ideas and significant issues from information texts. To enable children to identify issues shared by texts and compare the treatment of such issues. To foster discussion and questioning of information texts.

†† *Children working in pairs within a group.*

🕘 *20 minutes.*

Key background information

Traditional comprehension activities require children to answer set questions on texts; for each question there is generally a correct answer. This activity engages children in questioning each other; they start with a set of prompt questions but they are encouraged to probe responses and to ask follow-up questions of their own, dependent on the information that they obtain from their partners. The discussion centres on texts that deal with different but related issues, so that the readers are enabled to identify common issues and to compare and contrast the texts. This is an activity that can be done by a pair of groups (or one group subdivided) during guided or independent group work time.

Preparation

Read photocopiable pages 111–112 and answer the questions on photocopiable page 113 yourself. Make copies for each child. (Photocopiable page 113 provides both sets of questions. You will need to cut the sheet in half once you have made copies.) Try to anticipate what supplementary questions an interviewer might use in order to follow-up responses to these questions. If you do not wish to use the text provided on the photocopiable pages you will need to produce a similarly structured pair of texts and prompt questions more closely related to a topic of interest.

Resources needed

Photocopiable pages 111–113 or, alternatively, your own comprehension texts, paper, writing materials, highlighter pens.

What to do

Introduction

Explain to the group that half of them will be reading text A and half text B and that the texts provide information about similar but not identical issues. Also explain that they will be sharing the information that they have obtained by means of an interview, and that prompt questions will be provided. Make sure that the children know that they should use these questions systematically, but that they can query their partner's responses and ask questions of their own based on what their partners are telling them.

Development

Give half of the group photocopiable page 111 and the other half photocopiable pages 112, and allow them a suitable amount of time to read the text thoroughly, making marginal notes and highlighting points if necessary. The two halves of the group then pair up with each other and take it in turns to interview one another, asking questions about the text they have not read using the relevant prompt questions on photocopiable page 113 and their own supplementary questions to clarify responses or obtain any further information that they deem necessary. Interviewers can make notes as the interviewees respond. When both sets of partners have been interviewed, they should try to identify common issues in the texts.

Conclusion

Pairs should now swap texts and discuss any further information that they can derive from them. Conduct a shared writing activity in which you compose a summary of what has been learned, perhaps using a simple Venn diagram format (see illustration).

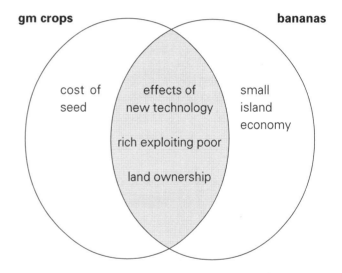

Suggestion(s) for extension

Extend this activity to looking at reports from different newspapers, extracts from different text books, and pieces of research writing that have been done by the children themselves about different aspects of the same topic.

Suggestion(s) for support

The activity can be conducted as a shared reading and writing activity, the teacher or another adult working with one half-group at a time before conducting a plenary in which both texts are read and compared.

Assessment opportunities

This activity should enable you to assess the children's independent reading capacity, their ability to derive main ideas from text and their ability to conduct a co-operative exchange of information.

Display ideas

The two texts and question sets can be displayed, including the children's annotations and highlighting, alongside the Venn diagrams or other summary formats.

Other aspects of the English PoS covered

Speaking and listening: 1a, b, c; 2a, b; 3a, b.
Writing 1a, b; 2a; 3a.

Reference to photocopiable sheets

Photocopiable pages 111 and 112 each provide a piece of information text. Photocopiable page 113 provides sets of related comprehension questions.

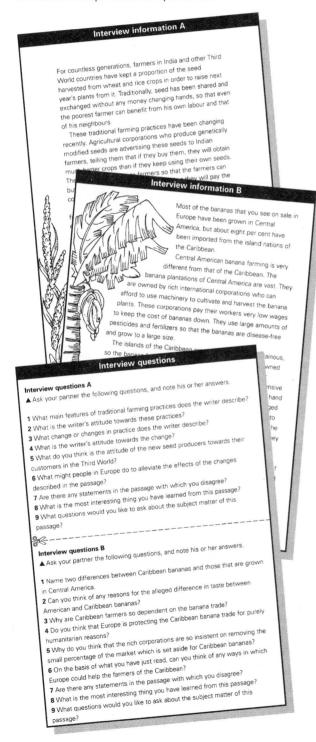

CONNECTIVES

To raise children's awareness of the role of different types of connective in signalling relationships between sentences and paragraphs.

†† *Whole-class introduction followed by small group work.*

🕐 *10 minutes whole-class work followed by 20 minutes follow-up.*

Key background information

Connectives, which are also known as conjunctives or sentence connectors, are words or phrases which signal important relationships between information presented in earlier sentences of a text and the information which is to follow.

Connectives are of four main types:

▲ Additive connectives introduce sentences which extend or reinforce the meaning of the sentences which have gone before.

Mammals give birth to live young. **Moreover***, they also suckle their young on milk produced by the mother.*

Other additive connectives are *furthermore, in other words, additionally, and.*

▲ Adversative connectives introduce sentences which present some sort of contrast with the given information.

Mammals give birth to live young. **However***, there are exceptions: both the echidna and the duck-billed platypus are egg-laying mammals.*

Other adversative connectives are *but, in spite of this, yet, nevertheless, on the other hand.*

▲ Causal connectives indicate that what follows is a result of what has gone before.

Mammals give birth to live young. **Consequently***, their maternal behaviour differs markedly from that of egg-laying animals.*

Other causal connectives are *because of this, so, hence, therefore, as a result.*

▲ Temporal connectives indicate time relationships between sentences.

Mammals give birth to live young. **Subsequently***, the young undergo a period in which they are reared by their parents.*

Other temporal connectives are *eventually, at last, suddenly, finally, earlier.*

Connectives are found in all types of writing, but in information texts they can be particularly important and problematical. This is because in certain types of non-narrative information books, there is a preponderance of more abstract causal and adversative connectives such as *consequently, furthermore, however, notwithstanding, hence* and *therefore.* Research into children's comprehension of these links has suggested that it is possible for children to understand the separate sentences in a text, but to be confused by the text as a whole because

of difficulties with the words and phrases that bind the sentences together.

This activity presents a set of routines by which you can gradually help children to understand connectives in their reading, and use them in their writing. It is a text- and sentence-level activity which would fit into the second 15 minutes of the Literacy Hour, following the shared reading of a non-fiction text.

Preparation

Collect a set of stem sentences (such as the *Mammals give birth to live young* example) which can be used with varying connectives to demonstrate the use of these words and phrases. Have a go at composing sentences which might typically follow the different types of connectives listed in 'Key background information'. Select or compose a text which exemplifies the use of some of these connectives. If you have composed the stem sentences and the text yourself, enlarge them for group reading. If you have taken them from published texts make sure that you have a photocopying licence before enlarging them. For the extension activity prepare cloze procedures for the children to complete from which the connectives have been deleted.

Resources needed

Stem sentences, an enlarged text, board/flip chart, strips of paper or card, Blu-Tack. For the extension activity – cloze procedures.

What to do

Introduction

Present a stem sentence to the class together with a choice of three connectives. For example:

Corporal punishment is illegal in all British schools.

However,

As a result of this,

In other words,

Add an appropriate completion to the sentences suggested by the connectives, and talk to the children about how the completion is necessitated by the choice of connective. You might reinforce this by swapping completions between connectives and talking about how the sentences 'feel' wrong.

Show the children another stem sentence with the same set of connectives and ask them to suggest their own completions. A good way of doing this is to treat this phase of the activity as a circle game, each child taking it in turn to offer a completion or saying 'pass'. Write particularly interesting completions up on the board, and afterwards talk about their common features with the class.

Development

Show the children the enlarged text and ask them to identify the connectives. Reiterate how these words function in context. Select one sentence and cover the portion of it following the connective with a strip of paper or card. Ask the children to compose an alternative completion which is in agreement with the connective, and preserves the integrity of the text. Repeat this process with other sentences in the text.

Conclusion

Return to the oral game and repeat it with other connectives from the 'four function' families. Ask children to look out for connectives in their own reading, and to offer them as starters for the oral activity in subsequent sessions.

Suggestion(s) for extension

Present more confident readers with cloze procedures from which connectives have been deleted, and ask them to supply appropriate words. This is a good way of introducing some of the less common logical connectives like 'hence' and 'thus'.

Suggestion(s) for support

The best way of supporting the learning of connectives is to play the oral game regularly, starting with familiar, narrative-type connectives such as *next, suddenly, in spite of this*. Progress gradually from fictional to historical and biographical narrative, and then to report texts which use the more abstract connectives.

Assessment opportunities

Observe the children's awareness of logical and temporal links between sentences, and their knowledge of the range of ways in which these links are represented by words and phrases.

Opportunities for IT

Using a word processor, children could compose their own texts using the different types of connectives. They could try to create a text that makes sense and uses all four families.

Display ideas

Stem sentences can be displayed with a range of alternative connectives as choice trees (see the diagrams below). The children could write various completions on pieces of moveable cards. These can then be placed in an envelope and the children can try out matching completions to the different connectives and test the results.

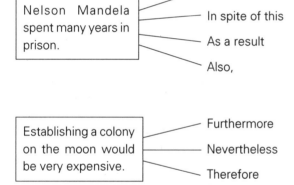

Other aspects of the English PoS covered

Speaking and listening: 1a, b, c; 2a; 3a. Writing: 1a, b; 2a; 3a.

PARAGRAPHING

To familiarize children with sentence sequences within paragraphs.

†† *Whole class or small group.*

🕐 *30–40 minutes.*

Key background information

Paragraphs are graphic devices for organizing information into segments of related sentences. The sentences within a paragraph are usually organized so that there is a topic sentence which expresses the main theme of the paragraph, accompanied by other sentences which expand on the topic sentence, or exemplify the statement that it makes, or argue against it. In this activity, a text has been divided into paragraphs which are organized in a very simple way. Each paragraph begins with the topic sentence, which is followed by three or four supporting sentences. The children's task is to reconstruct the text from the sentences, which will have been shuffled by the teacher first: to identify the topic sentences and their related supporting sentences, then to use cohesive ties in order to reconstruct the paragraphs and the order in which they occurred in the original passage.

The idea of paragraphing and sentence order within paragraphs can be introduced in the second part of the Literacy Hour. The sequencing work can be done in independent group work.

Preparation

Make copies of photocopiable page 114 onto thin card and cut it up into separate sentences. You will also need to make paper copies of this, one sheet for every three or four children. Make one enlarged copy for display with the class. Also make an enlarged copy of the photocopiable sheet, showing the sentences in the correct order. Alternatively, prepare a text more closely related to current concerns which shares the same sort of sentence sequence within its paragraphs. Find or compose a similar text containing the same number of sentences that can be shown to the children intact. Make an enlarged copy of this. Note that on photocopiable page 114, the topic sentences have been emboldened so that children can pick them out and use them as the nuclei for the other sentences. If you want to make the activity more challenging, so that the children have to decide for themselves which are the topic sentences, then you can retype these three sentences in plain letters. Prepare a simpler fiction passage for those children requiring support.

Resources needed

Photocopiable page 114 or an alternative text copied onto thin card and cut up into separate sentences, an uncut passage of approximately three or four paragraphs on the same topic, highlighter pens, board/flip chart. For the support activity – a simpler passage.

What to do

Introduction

Talk to the children about earthquakes or your own selected topic, eliciting their current knowledge by questioning, prompting and probing. Write significant words and phrases on the board. If the children are unfamiliar with some of the technical vocabulary used in the passage, you could introduce this in the course of the discussion. Alternatively, you could use this as an opportunity to teach the words in the context of the sequencing activity.

Show the children your uncut passage of three or four paragraphs on the same topic and ask them to identify the paragraphs. Conduct a shared reading and ask the children to think about why the author made breaks in the text at those particular points. Revisit each paragraph, conducting a simple content analysis of the sentences, and try to steer the children towards seeing that each paragraph groups a particular cluster of information points in a particular way.

Development

Give out the sentences from the photocopiable sheet, one set to a group of three or four children, and tell them that they can be rearranged into a passage of three paragraphs about earthquakes.

There are plenty of opportunities for providing different levels of support within this activity. You may decide to tell the children that the first two paragraphs each have three sentences and the third paragraph has four, related to earthquake origins, the epicentre and tidal waves, respectively. Using the emboldened topic sentences will facilitate the sorting process. Alternatively, you may keep initial support to a minimum. However, as children work, you should draw their attention to the cohesive ties in the passage. For example, a sentence containing the words 'these zones' must logically come after another sentence which introduces the concept of the zones. As children finish the sequencing activity, ask them to compare their reconstructions with those of other groups, and to discuss any differences.

Conclusion

Bring the whole group together and show them the enlarged version of the photocopiable sheet showing the sentences in the correct order. Discuss any differences

with their own reconstructions. Note that alternatives are possible. Use the highlighter pens to underline reference words like *this* and *these* and *it* and to draw lines which link them back to their referents. You can also underline vocabulary items related to the main idea of each paragraph (for example, in paragraph three, *seabed, displacement, water, waves, tidal wave, tsunamis,* and *coastal*).

Suggestion(s) for extension

The same process can be applied to more complex paragraphs. Show the children examples in which the topic sentence is in the middle or at the end of the paragraph, or where the other sentences argue against the topic sentences, or where all of the sentences are of equal status and the topic sentence is 'implicit'. Children can collect examples of these paragraphs and attempt to integrate their structures into their own writing.

Suggestion(s) for support

As mentioned in 'What to do', there is provision for support built into this activity. If you are working with less able children, use a simpler passage, perhaps beginning with fiction, where the temporal progression of narrative provides a less abstract structure. It is a good idea to model the process of sequencing, and to talk about what you are doing as you reorder the sentences, making your thinking audible to the children. Encourage them to do the same.

Assessment opportunities

Assess the children's awareness of the underlying structures in text, particularly cohesive devices such as reference and lexical patterns.

Opportunities for IT

The jumbled texts could be presented to the children on a word processor. The children can re-order them using the 'cut and paste' or 'drag and drop' facilities of the word processor. Once they think they have found the correct order the different sentences can be joined up to make a complete paragraph. This is a good time to ensure that the children know how to use the return key to split lines and the delete key at the start of the line to join them back up again. Make sure they realize that paragraphs are separated by an extra blank line, made by pressing the return key twice.

The final versions can be printed out and used for comparison and as a part of a class display. More able pupils could set up a text for other pupils to reorder.

Display ideas
Set up a board on which to display the sentences of shuffled paragraphs which children can reconstruct. Change the material frequently, and make sure that different types of paragraphs are represented. Intact paragraphs can be displayed alongside, with topic sentences highlighted and the relationships between sentences indicated graphically.

Other aspects of the English PoS covered
Speaking and listening: 1a, b, c; 2a, b; 3a, b.

Reference to photocopiable sheet
Photocopiable page 114 provides some text on earthquakes. The sentences in each paragraph are jumbled up by the teacher and the children must attempt to sort them into the correct order. Note that there are many different ways of reordering the sentences.

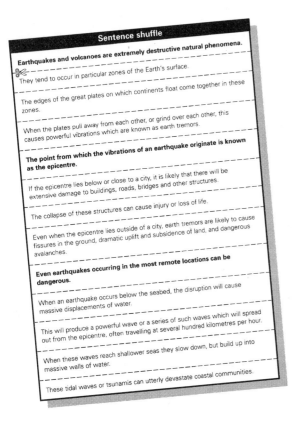

BELIEVE IT OR NOT

To enhance children's motivation to read a wide range of non-fiction. To provide a context for note taking, non-fiction reviewing and referencing. To be aware of some of the ways in which authors record and acknowledge their sources.

†† *Open-ended whole-class activity.*

🕐 *15 minutes introductory talk followed by open-ended activity.*

Key background information
Children at Key Stage Two are often enthusiastic collectors of various things, including abstruse facts which may or may not be linked to a range of personal enthusiasms. The aim of this activity is to channel this enthusiasm into a public forum for the sharing of facts which have been arrived at through recreational reading of non-fiction. The activity is inspired by the syndicated 'Believe it or not' column, once popular in the children's pages of newspapers, compiled by journalist George Ripley who travelled the world collecting bizarre facts.

This is an open-ended activity best done outside of the constraints of the Literacy Hour. Start it off in storytime and keep it going as a relaxation activity at the end of the morning or afternoon.

Preparation
Collect as many astonishing-fact type books as you can. Browse through them and create an A2 or A3 chart in which you present a selection of facts that you think will appeal to the class. These might be clustered around a particular topic, or they might be selected just for their novelty value. Good sources for this type of thing include the annual *Guinness Book of Records* and the *Horrible Histories* series (Scholastic). For each fact that you display, add a note or a numbered footnote identifying the source of the fact, using a formal referencing system such as Harvard (name of author, date of publication, title of publication, place of publication, publisher).

Resources needed
Fact books, a selection of facts, display materials.

What to do
Introduction
Show the children your chart and conduct a shared reading, prompting casual conversation about the selected facts as you do so. Then ask the children how they can be sure that these 'facts' are indeed facts. Draw the children's attention to the bibliographic information that you have provided, then show them the books that these details refer to, explaining how and why you have cited author, title, date and publication details. By doing this, you will have established that your information has been collated

from published books rather than invented, but it is important to emphasize that this does not in itself verify the information. The information is only as reliable as the book it was derived from. Stress that it is often necessary to look for confirmation from a range of sources.

Development

Explain to the children that you are going to invite them to expand the display over the course of a term or longer. The challenge is for each child to add at least one fact to the display every week, and to cite the details of the books from which they have taken the details. Invite the children to make suggestions as to how the information should be displayed – by topic or at random? Illustrated or not? You might give the children the choice of designing illustrated A4 or A5 fact formats using desktop publishing, or simply handwriting facts that they come by on Post-it notes. If you can get hold of some of the Ripley columns, this might supply some inspiration. (Children can write to the Ripley's Believe It or Not Museum in Orlando in Orange County, Florida, for further information, or visit their web site.) Suggest to the children that sources such as the *Guinness Book of Records* are an easy way of doing this, and that it is more rewarding to come up with interesting facts that are harder to come by.

Conclusion

Spend a few minutes every week reviewing and discussing additions to the display.

Suggestion(s) for extension

The activity can be spiced up by encouraging particularly creative individuals to add semi-plausible lies to the display, complete with fake references. (For example: Nests of ants have been known to communicate with human beings by swarming in patterns which represent letters of the alphabet. Phibbs, Matilda (1999) Wonders of Entomology. Gotham. Fake Educational Press). This can be done once a week, and the children asked to spot the lie during your review time.

With older and more confident readers, the display can be used to raise issues of reliability in non-fiction text. For example, are more modern sources more reliable than older ones? Are popular books, or those for younger readers, less reliable than specialist ones? This can be

linked to media issues by discussing how 'facts' presented in specialist journals are represented in the press (see the the previous activity in this chapter 'Formality and authority' on page 48).

Suggestion(s) for support

Start by asking the children about their personal interests, and encourage them to build up a collection of four or five facts related to something they know about – stress that they do not have to be 'spectacular' facts. Children could also be encouraged to ask members of their family to share facts about their work or their hobbies that might be of interest.

Assessment opportunities

Assess children's awareness of issues such as reliability and the importance of regarding purported facts critically. This activity should also provide information about reading range.

Opportunities for IT

The children could use a word processor to write their 'believe it or not' fact for the class display. They could use this opportunity to decide how best to present their specific fact for display. This might involve using different fonts, sizes, colours and organization of the text. They could also add suitable illustrations. Older or more able pupils could also be introduced to the idea of footnotes and shown how these work on more sophisticated word processors. Even if their word processor does not have this facility children can use smaller font sizes and italics to create the footnote or numbered references next to the text.

The children could also use CD-ROM encyclopaedias or the Internet to search out their facts for the class display. If run over a period of time it would give every child in the class an opportunity to find and present their fact using information and communications technologies.

Display ideas

The activity is built around a display to which the children will constantly be adding.

Other aspects of the English PoS covered

Speaking and listening: 1a, b, c; 2a, b; 3a, b.
Writing: 1a, b; 2a; 3a.

Poetry

Poetry is often regarded as either a purely recreational form of reading material, or a refined and precious medium which needs to be approached with awe and reverence. In this chapter, poetry is regarded as broader and more fundamental, encompassing texts in which an effort has been made both to strip language of redundancy and to play with its aesthestic qualities. The question of what makes a particular text poetic is addressed in a duly circumspect way in the opening activity. Pupils are then encouraged to explore poetic language in published texts, reflecting on their reading, and discussing and recording personal responses in a variety of ways. Having identified these language patterns, pupils are encouraged to use them to extend their own writing.

The chapter also includes activities which are intended to stimulate the reader's curiosity about aesthetic qualities of language and what seems to be an inherent tendency to play with the sounds and meanings of words. The relevance of this kind of metalinguistic amusement to literacy development has become increasingly clear in recent years, and its promulgation in the classroom is an essential counterpoise to the highly structured curriculum of the National Literacy Strategy.

WHAT MAKES A POEM A POEM?

To develop awareness of the poetic aspects of language.

†† *Whole-class introduction followed by whole-class or group development.*

🕐 *20–30 minutes with open-ended follow-up.*

Key background information

An apocryphal story tells of a child, when asked to define poetry, replying that it's a kind of writing in which the lines don't reach the right-hand side of the page. Every teacher has come across 'poems', either published or written by children, in which broken lineation appears to be the only 'poetic' quality. But if writing requires more than this in order to qualify as being poetic, what should this 'more' consist of? Traditionalists argue that classifying a piece of writing as a poem bestows a mark of honour which can only be earned by highly skilled refinement of language. Others argue that any form of memorable language can be regarded as poetic: if somebody regards it as a poem, then it is a poem.

There are complex issues here that you will not want to spend too much time on at Key Stage Two, but it is vital that children of this age are aware that a controversy does exist. At the very least, they should understand that while rhyme is optional, poetry requires more than just the reorganization of lines of prose. The introduction session to this activity can be conducted during the first segment of the Literacy Hour.

Preparation

Collect short examples and extracts from different types of poetry. These should cover rhyming and non-rhyming, narrative and non-narrative, traditional and modern. In the latter, try to include examples which traditionalists might argue against classifying as poetry. Some anthologists include Gerard Benson *This Poem Doesn't Rhyme* and Wes Magee *Madtail, Miniwhale and Other Shape Poems*. Draw up a list of criteria for yourself as to why these different examples should or should not be described as poetry. Mount a display using this material under the question 'Why is this poetry?' Provide a space in which the children can add their replies. Make sufficient copies of photocopiable page 115, one for each child, or make one enlarged copy for use with the whole class or group.

Resources needed

Poetry and display material as described in 'Preparation', writing materials, photocopiable page 115.

What to do

Introduction

Conduct a shared reading session using selected items from the display. Review any replies that the children have posted to your question and use these as stimuli for an initial discussion. If you have not had any replies, pose the question in relation to the reading, and share-write the children's responses. Probe, and offer counter-examples to, any responses that seem to offer too narrow or too vague criteria; for example, 'it has to rhyme'; 'it has to be funny'; 'the lines have to be a different length'.

Development

Next, either distribute individual copies of photocopiable page 115 or display the enlarged version. Conduct a shared or guided reading of this material, and pose the question: what distinguishes the poetry from the prose? Help the children to consider the following aspects of language:

▲ use of rhythm, rhyme, alliteration, onomatopoeia

▲ use of simile, metaphor, personification

▲ choice of vocabulary

▲ graphic organization of words and lines

▲ expression of emotion

▲ perspective of the writer

▲ economy of language (is there more 'redundancy' in prose?)

Note that this list is intended to provide a starting point for discussion rather than an attempt to identify rules for distinguishing poetry from prose.

Do not be tempted to formulate a definition of poetry! It is important to convince children that there are many questions in the field of literacy for which there will never be satisfactory answers. The important thing is to keep thinking about such questions.

Conclusion

If you have been working with a group, ask them to provide a summary of their discussion to the class. If you have been working with the whole class, elicit a share-written summary which can be added to the display.

Suggestion(s) for extension

The discussion of criteria can be used to inform the choices that children make in some of the activities that follow. It can also be used as a way of helping children to evaluate their own writing. More fluent readers can be encouraged to compile a personal anthology of examples of poetic language from a range of sources including conventional prose, non-fiction and the media. It should not be confined just to 'poems' but to any chunks of language that use words in a striking way.

Suggestion(s) for support

Carry out further exploration of more immediate types of poetic language such as nursery rhymes and narrative folk-songs. Compare these with their prose parallels, and discuss similarities and differences.

Assessment opportunities

Note the children's ability to identify less obvious aspects of poetic language, to engage in discussion based on close reading, and to relate insights to future reading and writing.

Display ideas

The display used to initiate discussion at the start of the activity can be expanded to include the children's summaries of the discussion. The children could also add their own poetry to the display, writing out the prose equivalent to go alongside it.

Other aspects of the English PoS covered

Speaking and listening: 1a, b, c; 2a, b; 3a, b.
Writing: 1a, b; 2a; 3a.

Reference to photocopiable sheet

Photocopiable page 115 gives three different styles of poem. Underneath each piece of poetry the prose equivalent has been written. The children must read the texts and consider what it is that differentiates the poetry from the prose, and what it is that enables a poem to be defined as such.

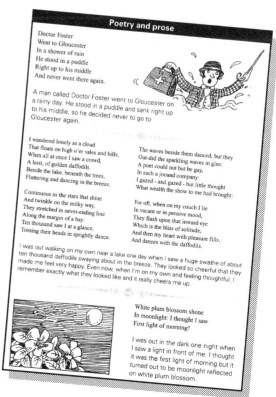

A COMMUNITY ANTHOLOGY

To raise awareness of the role that poetry and poetic language play in everyday life and in the memories of ordinary people. To create a class anthology of favourite poems.

†† *Whole-class extended project.*

🕐 *15–20 minute introduction then open-ended follow-up.*

Key background information

Most adults, if pressed, can recite a poem or a fragment of a poem that they learned when younger. (Poetry is defined very broadly here, and might include items such as playground verses, nursery rhymes, epitaphs, football chants, rude verses, advertising jingles or refrains from popular songs.) The universality of this ability is evidence of the power of memorable language, especially if reinforced by rhythm and rhyme. This activity is aimed at increasing children's curiosity about poetic language by encouraging them to investigate its appeal to a wide range of people. The shared reading in the Literacy Hour can be done during the first 15 minutes of the Literacy Hour.

Preparation

Ask each member of the school staff, including ancillary staff and volunteers, to contribute a 'poem' or poetic fragment that they learned when younger. Ensure that you make it clear that you are not just interested in well-respected classics, and try to include items from the categories listed above. Ask each contributor when and where they learned the piece, and why they think they have retained it in their heads and hearts. Using a word processor, type each piece in a version large enough to be read by the class, and make an initial stimulus display of them. You should also, with permission, type out the names of the contributors and their thoughts on why their particular piece has been personally significant for them, but you should not disclose this information until the taught session.

Resources needed

Display as described in 'Preparation'.

What to do

Introduction

Conduct a shared reading of a selection of the poems and fragments on display, and engage the children in discussion about them, asking them what they think the various appeal of these pieces might be, for example original use of words, vivid imagery, and so on.

Development

Tell the children where you got the pieces from, and ask the children to guess who contributed each. After some discussion, attach names and statements to each piece, and conduct a shared reading of the completed display. Ask the children to project themselves into their own futures and to try to anticipate what they will be carrying around within themselves in ten, twenty or thirty years time.

Conclusion

Explain to the children that this is the start of a term or half-term project in which they will be expanding the display to include items contributed by their own families. Make sure that the children appreciate the breadth of items that you are interested in. Explain that they should also try to collect a statement from each contributor giving reasons as to why a particular item is significant. There is no need for this to be written, as you or the children can type up oral statements, but obviously it is preferable if they are in the words of the contributor. Stipulate a set time for class sharing of contributions.

Suggestion(s) for extension

This activity can be extended to other classes within the school who can also be asked to quiz family members about the poems they have retained, and can include languages other than English. It can also be used as a stimulus for communication between schools and between countries, perhaps using e-mail as a medium.

Suggestion(s) for support

The anthology can be used as the basis for group recitation, using enlarged versions of the most popular contributions.

Assessment opportunities

Assessment in the sense of judging literacy ability is not applicable for this playful, non-academic activity, but children's reactions to the poems might give you an insight into their appreciation of language.

Opportunities for IT

The children could present their own oral contributions using a word processor or desktop publishing package. They could type in their poem and the contributor's statement and then decide how to present this for the class display. They might, for example, present the contributor's comments in a different font, size or colour, or put the poem into a frame. Once items are moved from the display to a class anthology they may need to re-present them in a different format. This final process will mean children will need to retrieve their original work from where they have stored it, rework it and also save their new version.

Display ideas

Change the contributions on the display regularly, but keep older items in a special class anthology. The display can be embellished with visual material related to contributions, such as old school photographs and newspapers, pictures of pop-groups or football teams, rules for playground games and so on.

Other aspects of the English PoS covered

Speaking and listening: 1a, b, c, d; 2a, b; 3a, b, c.

DUAL-ENTRY DIARY

To help children to select lines, verses or longer extracts from poems that they find particularly interesting. To record their reflections on these extracts in writing. To discuss their selections and reflections with other readers.

†† *Whole class initially, then small group or individual work.*

⏲ *15 minute introduction; 20 minutes for children to work independently or in groups.*

Key background information

The dual-entry diary – this is simply a notebook with two columns per page, one for quotations and one for the diarist's comments on those quotations – can be an effective way of helping children to focus on the exact words used by a writer, while at the same time formulating individual responses to these words.

Dual-entry diary work can be conducted as a regular activity for groups working independently during the guided/independent phase of the Literacy Hour.

Preparation

Rehearse the activity by reading through one of your favourite poems. Select words, phrases or larger chunks that you deem to be particularly striking and copy them out verbatim in the left-hand column of a piece of paper that you have folded down the middle. After you have read the poem a couple of times, write in the right-hand column your thoughts concerning the extracts you have chosen. What do they make you think of? Enlarge what you have written. If you have a photocopying licence, make an enlarged version of another poem for shared reading. Also prepare an enlarged blank response sheet on which the children's reactions to the second poem can be written.

Resources needed

Your original poem, the enlarged response sheet, an enlarged version of another poem for shared reading, a blank response sheet, notebooks, writing materials.

What to do

Introduction

Read your original poem to the class and ask them to think about it and share their thoughts with a partner, then conduct a brief discussion of their responses. Next, show them the enlarged version of your response sheet and explain how you created it, stressing that one column consists of verbatim extracts from the poem, while the other expresses the thoughts and feelings that these words evoked in you. Ask the children to think and talk about which words they would have selected from the poem, and what they might have written as responses in the right-hand column.

Development

Conduct a shared reading of the second poem, and show the children the enlarged response sheet. Give the children time to think about the poem on their own, then ask four or five of the children to select words, phrases or larger chunks that particularly appealed to them. Write these out verbatim, and as you do so, ask each contributor to verbalize their thoughts and feelings about the selected extract. Write these in the right-hand column.

Conclusion

Distribute the notebooks and explain to the children that the procedure you have generated is one that they can use in order to help them reflect on the poetry that they read. The notebooks should serve as dual-entry diaries which will be both a record of the poetry reading that children do on their own, and a way of recording and comparing their reflections on their reading.

Suggestion(s) for extension

The dual-entry diary procedure can be extended to the reading of fiction and non-fiction texts. Notebooks can be used as the basis for an in-depth discussion of individual responses to reading.

Suggestion(s) for support

The activity can be conducted on a regular basis through shared reading and writing until children feel confident enough to take the activity over as independent individuals.

Assessment opportunities

Dual-entry diaries will provide some evidence of reading range, and of the readers' developing ability to formulate individual responses to their reading.

Display ideas

Share-written responses to poems which the whole class have read can form part of a poetry display.

Other aspects of the English PoS covered

Speaking and listening:1a, b, c.
Writing: 1a; 2a, b.

CHORAL READING

To enhance children's awareness of the power of the spoken word in relation to poetry. To select, prepare and perform a poem.

**†† ** *Whole class, followed by group work.*
**⏲ ** *One hour.*

Key background information

Like most literature, the roots of poetry are in the oral tradition. Many of the aspects of poetry that have already been discussed are essentially phonological, and have to be actually heard or recited to be fully appreciated. This activity involves children in appreciating how earlier readers have interpreted poems orally, and in making their own choices about how to perform their own favourite poems. Initial sharing can be done in the first 15 minutes of the Literacy Hour, group work in the 20-minute block and performance in the 10-minute final plenary.

Preparation

Make a collection of taped poetry. This should be a mixture of commercially published material, and tapes that have been made by the school community. Ensure that you include performances featuring choral readings of poems or parts of poems. Select extracts that you think will particularly appeal to the children you teach.

Over the course of a couple of weeks before the taught session, play the children selections from the taped collection. If you have a photocopying licence, make enlarged versions of the poems for the children to read while they are listening to them. Talk to the children about how the readers have interpreted the printed word, and ask them to think of ways in which they would like to interpret their own favourite poems.

Resources needed

Your tape collection, a mini-anthology of poems suitable for choral recitation, these might include: 'Calico Pie', by Edward Lear; 'The Computer's First Christmas Card' by Edwin Morgan; 'The ABC' by Spike Milligan; 'Tom Bone', by Charles Causley; 'The Crooked Man' by Ian Serailler; 'Spell of Creation' by Kathleen Raine; 'Night Mail', by WH Auden; 'Wha me mudder do', by Grace Nicholls. If you have a photocopying licence, make an enlarged version of the poem you have selected to read to the class.

What to do

Introduction

Read aloud a poem which has been popular with the class and ask the children to think of ways in which it might be read aloud by more than one voice, prompting them with extracts from poems read in this manner. Show the children an enlarged version of the poem and, using their suggestions, mark the poem with a coding system to indicate possibilities: for example, alternate lines to be read by halves of the class, the chorus to be read by a single person or the whole class; individual members of the class to read a line each, and so on. Experiment with two or three suggestions and show how underlining, highlighting and notes can be used to indicate decisions about how parts of the poem should be read.

Development

Divide the class into groups and give them a poem each to interpret. Allow them fifteen minutes to work out ways in which it might be presented and to decide on one of these ways to present to the class. Allow another ten minutes for rehearsal of the chosen version. This is best done in an area such as the school hall where the groups will have plenty of room to thrash things out without disturbing each other too much.

Conclusion

Each group takes it in turn to present their version to the whole class. Listeners can be encouraged to make appreciative or constructively critical comments.

Suggestion(s) for extension

Oral recitation can be accompanied by drama or music. Individuals or pairs of pupils can be commissioned to prepare 'productions' of longer poems which involve the participation of other members of the class. These can then be performed to the rest of the school in an assembly.

Suggestion(s) for support

Engaging less able readers in choral readings of poems that they have enjoyed when read aloud is a good way of enhancing appreciation of these poems and adding them to the store of texts that such readers can feel confident about during shared reading. Children can make personal anthologies of such poems.

Assessment opportunities

This activity should provide evidence of the children's ability to read aloud with appropriate expression.

Opportunities for IT

Shorter choral readings could be recorded using a microphone connected to the computer. The resulting audio file (which can be very large) could be used in a class multimedia presentation, possibly displaying the text of the poem with the choral reading in the background (like a talking book).

Other aspects of the English PoS covered

Speaking and listening: 1a, b, c, d; 2a, b; 3a, b, c.

LEARNING POEMS BY HEART

To enhance appreciation of personally chosen poems. To develop confidence in public speaking. To learn a favourite poem by heart.

†† *Whole class introduction, spread over a number of days; individual follow-up.*

⊕ *5 or 10 minutes a day for a week or two, followed by open-ended work by individual children.*

Key background information

Some older readers of this book might foster grim memories of being made to memorize poems, lacking in personal appeal and enforced upon them by teachers. Others might have fonder memories, and feel grateful that their schooldays equipped them with the ability to savour favourite poems without the help of a book. The key difference is in the attitude to the poem. The activity 'A community anthology' on page 66 may have demonstrated that most people find it difficult not to memorize some items of poetic language, as long as those items have personal significance. The challenge is in finding examples of good poetry that you can transfer your enthusiasm about to individuals or groups. Once this has been achieved, most children will take pride in committing such poems to memory.

Memorized poems can be recited as a stimulus to reading or the start of the Literacy Hour, or can be part of the sharing during the plenary.

Preparation

Return to the activity 'A community anthology' (see page 66) and select some of the memorized poems that the class particularly enjoyed. Also, think about poems that you know by heart yourself. If you do not know any such poems, choose a couple of short favourites and ensure that you have them memorized before proceeding with the activity. Ask for volunteers from your original contributors who are willing to recite memorized poems to the class, and assign them a date for their performances. Compile an anthology or display of poems that will appeal to the class and which you think might be relatively easy to memorize. (You may like to refer to the poems suggested in the preceding activity on page 68.)

Resources needed

Poems and people as described above. Poems and stories from the bardic tradition – versions of 'Beowulf', Nordic and Greek myths, and stories from the traditions of Africa, America, Asia and Australasia are widely available.

What to do

Introduce the activity by telling children about the earliest poets – the bards of many cultures across the world who carried poems and stories about inside their heads before the invention of writing. Familiarize the children with some examples of such poems or of the stories that have been derived from them.

Show the children the anthology or display that you have prepared and allow them time to browse through it and select poems that they like. Introduce your volunteer speakers to the class at strategic intervals, and let them perform, allowing time for the children to question them afterwards.

Explain to the children that you would like them to select poems to memorize and then perform. However, children should be persuaded rather than coerced to select poems for memorizing. When to attempt recitation, and whom to recite to, should also be matters of choice. Encourage children to memorize poems in manageable chunks, assisted by a 'response partner' equipped with the written version who can listen and prompt.

Once such choices have been made, it can be motivating to prepare and post a theatre-type programme detailing who is going to perform what, where and when.

Suggestion(s) for extension

Children can collate poems that they have managed to memorize in personalized anthologies. A class tape of children reciting poems can also be made and shared with other classes.

Suggestion(s) for support

Learning short, enjoyable poems by heart can be an effective strategy for enabling less able readers to associate familiar patterns of spoken language with their printed equivalents. The repetition inherent in much poetry makes it a particularly powerful medium in this respect, but only if the poems are learned truly by heart rather than by rote. The anxiety and drudgery of being forced to memorize and recite poems against one's will is guaranteed to make the reluctant reader even more reluctant.

Assessment opportunities

Note the children's readiness to select poems, and the oral skills that they exhibit when reciting them.

Display ideas

The written versions of the memorized poems can be displayed alongside illustrations and comments by the children as to why they selected them. Photographs of the children reciting them aloud can also be used.

Other aspects of the English PoS covered

Speaking and listening: 1a, b, c, d; 2a, b; 3a, b, c.

MYSTERIOUS POETRY

To encourage individual reflections on poems. To enhance awareness of how writers create a sense of uncertainty in readers.

†† *Whole class with individual follow-up.*

🕐 *15 minute introduction, open-ended follow-up.*

Key background information

A common feature of many poems is that they create a sense of uncertainty in the reader. This is not referring to the 'I haven't a clue what it's about' reaction which greets a lot of poetry, but to the feeling that the poet is creating an atmosphere which suggests certain events without explicitly stating them. (Walter de la Mare's 'The Listeners' is one of the best-known examples of this type of poetry.) Children often enjoy speculating about such poems, and this sort of investigation can help them to realize that some of the most interesting examples of literature are ones in which the reader has to make their own interpretations of what the writer has offered as a starting point.

Reading and comprehension of the two poems on photocopiable page 116 can be done during the first 15 minutes of the Literacy Hour.

Preparation

Make a collection of poems that evoke a sense of mystery and uncertainty. (The following anthologies should help.) *Otherworlds* compiled by Judith Nicholls (Faber), *The Puffin Book of Magic Verse*, edited by Charles Causley, *The Magic Tree*, edited by David Woolger (OUP). If you have a photocopying licence, prepare enlarged copies of selections that you think will appeal to your class. Present these as a display with the question 'What is this about?' Read the two poems on photocopiable page 116 and consider possible interpretations of them. The Stevenson poem is the more accessible of the two: it presents a strong visual and auditory image and simply requires the reader to think about who the horseman is and what he is up to. The Carroll poem, is more complex: by using a plethora of pronouns which do not have specified people to refer to, the poet creates possibilities for all sorts of

interpretations. Make an enlarged copy for use with the whole class.

Resources needed

A collection of poems as described in 'Preparation', photocopiable page 116, paper, writing materials.

What to do

Incorporate readings from your displayed collection into your daily read-aloud sessions. Encourage the children to speculate about what the poet was thinking and feeling when the poem was written.

Present the class with the two poems on photocopiable page 116, and conduct a shared reading of them. After reading each poem, ask the children the question: *What do you think this poem was about?* Allow the children five minutes to jot down their immediate reactions, then ask them to share their responses.

As a follow-up, ask the children to consider how the poet manages to create the atmosphere of mystery. Look at vocabulary, specific words and so on. Stress that there are no right or wrong interpretations of the poems. Ask the children to look out for similar poems in their own reading to share with the class.

Suggestion(s) for extension

Introduce children to the suggested anthologies in order to extend the range of such poems that they read. After writing down immediate reactions, children should work with a partner in order to identify the devices that the poet uses in order to create the atmosphere.

Suggestion(s) for support

Encourage children who find it difficult to write to formulate an immediate reaction through drawing. It is sometimes a good idea to give all children this option in order to diversify responses and to avoid stigmatizing graphic responses.

Assessment opportunities

Note the children's ability to verbalize individual responses to poems, and to identify rhetorical devices used by writers to create effects.

Display ideas

Display a variety of graphic and written responses to poems alongside the original text.

Other aspects of the English PoS covered

Speaking and listening: 1a, b, c, d; 2a, b; 3a.

Reference to photocopiable sheet

Photocopiable page 116 provides two poems which are read to the children and used to stimulate discussion.

NARRATIVE POEMS

To enhance children's appreciation of narrative poetry through discussion, visualization and inference.

†† *Whole class and individual or pair work.*

⏱ *Several sessions of about 30 minutes each.*

Key background information

Narrative poetry might well be the oldest genre of poetry, originating before the invention of writing when bards recited memorized stories, using rhythm and figurative language in order to make their recitations more fascinating and easier to commit to memory. Involving children in poems that tell stories is a good way of making a link between the familiar genre of prose narrative and the types of language that characterize poetry.

Sharing of the whole poem can be done during the first 15 minutes of the Literacy Hour.

Preparation

Make a collection of vivid narrative poems that you think might appeal to your class. *The Oxford Book of Story Poems* (edited by Christopher Stuart-Clark, Oxford University Press) is a good source. Select one poem that you particularly like. It should be long enough to read in daily instalments for a week or so, in order to build up a sense of anticipation. Preferably, it should also be a poem with a sense of mystery, lending itself to discussion and to a variety of interpretations of events. Browning's 'Pied Piper of Hamelin' might be a good choice for younger children, and Tennyson's 'Lady of Shallot' for older ones. Both of the poems have a strong narrative thread and are rich in imagery and a sense of mystery. If you have a photocopying licence, make an enlarged copy for class reading.

Familiarize yourself thoroughly with the selected poem and try to visualize the story that it tells. Write down any unanswered questions raised by the poem and entertain some possible answers to them.

Resources needed

Your selected poem, writing, drawing, painting and collage materials.

What to do

Introduction

Read the poem in instalments. Before each reading, invite the children to close their eyes and to visualize the unfurling events, as if they were watching in an interior cinema. After each reading, invite the children to speculate on what might happen next, and to discuss possible answers to unanswered questions. For example: *Where did the Pied Piper actually come from? Why was the Lady of Shallot confined to the island?*

Development

Devote one session to reading, summarizing and discussing the whole of the poem, using your enlarged version. Tell the children that they are now going to work on creating a class depiction of the story, with each child or pair working on one particular section. You might like to use the analogy of the Bayeaux Tapestry, but stress that you are looking for a variety of individual or pair responses, rather than one uniform style for the whole story. Allow individuals or groups to choose which section or sections they want to work on, and the media that they will use. Before they start the visual work, encourage them to handwrite verbatim their chosen section.

As the work develops, ask the children to write notes about their interpretations of the story, focusing on the questions that you discussed during your readings. At the end of the period you have allocated to the project, each child or pair should have created a picture and a set of speculations about the mysteries embedded in the poem.

Conclusion

Display the completed pictures as a narrative 'tapestry', with the appropriate handwritten sections of the poem under each picture, and the children's speculations about the poem alongside. Devote some time to allowing the children to view each other's work, and to talk about the many points at which their interpretations will have differed.

Suggestion(s) for extension

Independent readers can apply this procedure to non-narrative poetry, perhaps incorporating graphic responses into their dual-entry diaries (see the activity 'Dual-entry diary' on page 67).

Suggestion(s) for support

Start the project with a shorter narrative poem which is rich in visual imagery and mystery. (Edward Lear's 'The Jumblies' would be a good classic choice.) Invite children to select, write out, memorize and illustrate a favourite stanza.

Assessment opportunities

Visual, and very personal, interpretations of poetry are not really amenable to academic assessment.

Opportunities for IT

The class could make an electronic presentation of their completed narrative. This could be done using multimedia authoring software or as a set of world wide web pages. Software such as *Textease*, allows linked pages to be created and then saved as HTML, the format for web pages.

The children could type on the word processor their part of the poem and their thoughts about it, while their pictures could be scanned to make a digital image. These could then be presented together; maybe with a reading of the poem made by using a microphone attached to the computer.

This type of work requires careful planning at the outset to create a structure for the presentation that enables all of the different sections to be linked together. The work is often best undertaken when there is extra support in the classroom to work with each group as they prepare their own pages within the pre-determined structure.

Display ideas
This activity is built around the creation of a display which you may like to invite other classes in to view.

Other aspects of the English PoS covered
Speaking and listening: 1a, b, c, d; 2a, b; 3a, b.
Writing: 1a, b, c; 2a, b; 3a.

METAPHOR

To make children more aware of the role of metaphor in poetic and other types of writing.
†† *Whole class.*
🕐 *30 minutes.*

Key background information
Metaphor is the process by which an idea is intensified by providing an implicit comparison with another idea. 'That boy is a vacuum cleaner when he gets near food' does not imply that the boy actually turns into a domestic appliance, but it does serve to emphasize his healthy appetite. A closely related idea is simile, where the comparison is made explicit through the use of words such as 'like' and 'as'. 'That boy sucks in food like a vacuum cleaner'; 'That boy is as voracious as a vacuum cleaner.' Simile, as in this activity, is often regarded as a specific type of metaphor. Metaphor may be confusing to children if they are accustomed to constructing a literal mental picture of what they read. Helping them to appreciate metaphor is likely to enhance their enjoyment of reading and may help to improve their writing.

This activity focuses on the use of thematic metaphor in one of Shakespeare's best-known plays, but the procedure can be easily adopted to simpler subject matter. Investigations into metaphor could be an activity within the 20-minute block of the Literacy Hour.

Preparation
Read or view 'Macbeth' in one of the versions mentioned below. Collect examples of metaphors from your own reading, and from books and other texts that you have shared with the class. Draw the children's attention to metaphors in the course of everyday reading and talking activities and ask them to find examples to share with the class during the activity. Make copies of photocopiable page 117, one for each child.

Resources needed
A version of 'Macbeth' accessible to your pupils, such as the *Animated Shakespeare* video version, or the *Lamb's Tales from Shakespeare*, Charles and Mary Lamb (Puffin Classics), or the recent retelling from Macdonald Press, retold by Bruce Colville; quotations from 'Macbeth', including those on photocopiable page 117.

What to do
Read or watch 'Macbeth' with your class, and allow plenty of time for discussion and for activities such as responding through the use of a dual-entry diary, memorizing and reciting quotations from it, and creating pictures.

Distribute copies of photocopiable page 117 and ask the children to recall the episodes from which these lines have been taken. Discuss any unfamiliar vocabulary, and ask the children to visualize the processes depicted by the lines. Ask the children to try to describe how the image evoked makes the process more vivid. For example, what more do we experience by reading the simile in the final quotation than we would from a statement such as 'Macbeth must be afraid that he's going to lose his title'? Try to relate this to the children's broader reading, providing them with examples of the metaphors you have collected from books that you have read aloud with the class. Ask the children to contribute examples that they have found themselves.

You could also ask the children whether they can spot the underlying theme uniting the different metaphors. Why do they think a writer would choose a particular theme for unifying metaphors in a piece of writing?

Suggestion(s) for extension

Children could also be asked to look out for examples of metaphorical themes in their own reading.

You could also ask children to think about how a metaphor, invented to sharpen language and perception, can lose its power by overuse and turn into a cliché. A good contemporary example might be the use of the word 'brilliant' as a term of approbation. Originally based on a metaphorical connection between an everyday event and stellar radiance, this word has now lost much of its power.

Suggestion(s) for support

Precede the activity with a survey of metaphors in everyday speech, perhaps linked to a display. For example, what do we mean when we describe somebody as 'a bookworm', or 'a misery guts', or 'a ray of sunshine', or 'a star'? Common idioms, such as 'pushing up daisies', 'got out of bed on the wrong side', 'got on like a house on fire' and 'a wolf in sheep's clothing' are metaphors whose poetic and visual qualities have been blunted by familiarity. By analysing their possible origins and pictorial qualities, children can be made aware of the power of fresher metaphors in their reading and writing.

Assessment opportunities

Note children's awareness of the effects of figurative writing, and their ability to identify examples in their own reading.

Display ideas

Metaphors collected from reading and from everyday speech can be displayed with notes about their sources.

Other aspects of the English PoS covered

Speaking and listening: 1a, b, c, d; 2a, b, c; 3a, b.

Reference to photocopiable sheet

Photocopiable page 117 provides a number of metaphors from 'Macbeth'. The children consider how the use of metaphor makes the processes or activities being described more vivid to the reader.

COMPOUNDS, COINAGES AND KENNINGS

To explore the metaphorical aspects of morphology.

†† *Whole class followed by group or individual work.*

🕑 *15 minutes introduction followed by 20–40 minutes follow-up.*

Key background information

Compound words are those in which two ideas are welded together into one. The new meaning thus created can be quite transparent (eggcup, headlouse, wristwatch) or a touch metaphorical (redhead, lowlife, dragonfly). Compound meanings that were once transparent, such as cupboard and wardrobe (a board on which cups were hung; protection for one's robes) are now less so. An interesting type of historical compound is the kenning;

abbreviated metaphors that were common in Anglo-Saxon poetry (a river referred to as a swan lane; the body as the bone house). This activity encourages children to investigate the structure of such words, and to invent their own.

Preparation

Start to make a collection of compound words, starting with those on photocopiable page 118. Make a display of these, sorting them into transparent compounds and those which have a metaphorical element. Draw the children's attention to compounds in reading and speech, and invite them to add any that they find to the display. Make copies of photocopiable page 118, one for each child.

Resources needed

Photocopiable page 118, dictionaries, writing materials, paper, an etymological dictionary for reference.

What to do

Introduction

Show the children the display you have created and draw their attention to the anatomy of the words and the different types of compounds. Invite them to speculate on the origins of the less transparent compounds before demonstrating the use of the etymological dictionary in order to check their hypotheses. Introduce the term 'kennings' and provide them with some examples of this device.

Development

Distribute photocopiable page 118 and ask the children to browse through the alphabetical list with a partner, discussing the origins of the words. Give out the dictionaries as well, and ask the children to browse through them, working to a strict time-limit, in order to find other examples which they can then add to the photocopiable sheet. Next, invite them to complete the list of surreal coinages, permuting elements from the words in the table and adding others if they like. On a separate sheet of paper they should try to make up a definition for each coinage, perhaps illustrating a selection with pictures and example sentences. The list of kennings can also be extended during this session or as a separate activity.

Conclusion

Ask the children to share their invented words with the rest of the class.

Suggestion(s) for extension

Encourage children to incorporate coinages and kennings into their own creative writing. Ask them to think of other compound words and to consider their origins. The use of etymological dictionaries can be extended to investigate word origins other then compounds.

The study of word structure can also move beyond compounds into the field of complex words consisting of roots and affixes.

Suggestion(s) for support

Help less able readers to identify the separate elements in compound words by asking them to draw diagrams of the meaning of the compound with the word parts separated out as labels. For example, a wrist wearing a watch.

Assessment opportunities

Note the children's awareness of word structure, and their confidence and creativity in using word structure flexibly to create their own meanings.

Display ideas

The initial stimulus display can be extended using the children's own discoveries, inventions and illustrations.

Other aspects of the English PoS covered

Speaking and listening: 1a, b, c, d; 2a, b; 3a, b.
Writing: 1a, b, c; 2a; 3a.

Reference to photocopiable sheet

Photocopiable page 118 lists some compound words. Using these as stimulus, the children must attempt to combine the words to create other compounds. The sheet also requires the children to create some kennings.

Compounds, coinages and kennings

Compounds
▲ Can you find some other compound words to add to this list?

anteater	newspaper
buttercup	overboard
candlestick	penfriend
dragonfly	quagmire
eggcup	railway
farmhouse	sunrise
greyhound	teacake
hedgehog	underpants
inkwell	vineyard
jamjar	woodworm
kneecap	xylophone
lighthouse	yearbook
molehill	zigzag

Compound coinages
▲ These compounds are made up words. Make up some more yourself and write definitions for them.

antworm
butterphone
candlepants

Kennings
▲ Make up some kennings of your own.

ant —— stingswarmer
bee —— honeyguts

FROM NON-FICTION TO POETRY

To help children to identify main ideas in a descriptive passage and the words and phrases that express them. To identify redundant words and phrases. To find similes, metaphors and related words and phrases to elaborate main ideas.

✝✝ *Individuals or pairs, working in a small group or as a whole class. It is particularly effective as an activity done by two or three children working together at a word processor.*

🕐 *30–45 minutes.*

Key background information

In normal prose, there is a large amount of redundancy – many of the words are not strictly necessary for the conveyance of information. This is evident when we compare normal prose with information that has been reduced to telegraphic form or to a set of notes. Poetic language is often characterized by a different type of 'condensed language': the poet selects just enough words to convey the maximum amount of meaning to the reader.

In this activity, the children take normal prose and reduce it to its bare essentials before attempting to intensify the impact of the remaining words by creating related ideas and putting them into a poetic form.

The introduction could comprise the first 15 minutes of the Literacy Hour. Working from prose to poetry could fit into a 20-minute block and the sharing of poems could be done in the final 10-minute plenary session.

Preparation

Find three or four information texts on different subjects whose content you think will appeal to the children doing the activity. Some of the texts provided as photocopiable pages in the previous chapter might be suitable, for example the elephant's trunk text on photocopiable page 107 or the Chernobyl text on photocopiable page 106.

In the first instance, they should not be longer than 200–300 words. Go through one of the texts yourself and highlight what you think the most important words and phrases are. Write these out on a separate piece of paper and play about with their order, substituting synonyms and inserting related words and phrases, until you have a piece of writing that is your own.

Resources needed

Information texts as specified in 'Preparation'. A separate collection consisting of an information text, a related poem (haiku are useful, but this is not a haiku writing activity), a telegraphic message and notes made from a description. This range of different texts should cover the same content. (The texts on the hummingbird provided on photocopiable page 124 could be used for this.) Thin cards. A word processor or, if the activity is being done on paper, highlighter pens, a dictionary and thesaurus.

What to do

Introduction

Conduct a shared reading of the model texts with the children (the poem, the telegraph message and the notes). Discuss the differences between them, focusing on the idea of redundancy and condensed language. Return to the normal prose text and ask the children to identify the main ideas in it. This may require careful questioning and demonstration. For example: *What is the most important thing the writer is trying to tell you here?*

Help the children to identify the key words and phrases which express these ideas. Show the children how to emphasize these ideas by either highlighting the key words and phrases, or striking out redundant ones. Copy the words and phrases onto cards and demonstrate the process you went through when you were preparing the activity, talking through alternative reorderings and the use of additional words and phrases, including similes and metaphors. Encourage the children to contribute to this reshaping, and to decide when a satisfactory presentation has been produced.

Development

Present the children with a choice of text, preferably as a file saved in a word-processing package. (This will enable other children to use the same text without you having to create a fresh file when the original has been reshaped into a poem.) If necessary, show the children how they can highlight aspects of the text and use the delete, drag, and cut and paste functions to manipulate the original text. The use of the programme's thesaurus to find synonyms and related words should also be demonstrated – this function is best used in conjunction with a conventional dictionary.

Working in twos or threes, the children should aim to produce a poem, inspired by the original text and conveying the same ideas, but embellished and personalized by their own additions and reorderings.

Conclusion
Ask children to present their completed poems to the class and talk about the language choices that they have made. Different poems based on the same original text might be particularly rich sources for discussion.

Suggestion(s) for extension
The introductory session of this activity can be revisited when children are reading information texts and learning to take notes.

Suggestion(s) for support
The entire activity can be conducted as shared reading and writing.

Assessment opportunities
Note the children's ability to identify main ideas, and to paraphrase and express these ideas through choices of vocabulary.

Display ideas
Display the original text with a selection of the children's poetic paraphrases.

Other aspects of the English PoS covered
Speaking and listening: 1a, b, c; 2a; 3a.
Writing: 1a, b; 2a; 3a.

ONSET AND RIME ONOMATOPOEIA GENERATORS

To enable children to practise blending skills by using a matrix to permutate onsets and rimes. To reflect on the aesthetic qualities of the words that they create. To engage in creative writing to assign meanings to these words.

†† *Small group.*

🕐 *10–15 minutes of intensive work followed by open-ended follow-up.*

Key background information
Any syllable or monosyllabic word can be segmented into an onset and a rime. The onset consists of any letters that occur before the vowel, and the rime of the vowel and any letters that follow it. (Syllables or monosyllabic words that begin with a vowel consist only of rimes.) Much recent work on early reading has suggested that a crucial role is played by onset and rime awareness, and by the ability to blend onsets and rimes into syllables and words. This activity is designed to provide a playful and creative context for developing onset and rime awareness and blending skill in early readers at Key Stage Two.

However, the activity can also be used to enhance the sensitivity of all readers to the aesthetic qualities of sound combinations within words. It has often been pointed out that the sounds of particular onsets and rimes seem to generate meaning associations in listeners' minds. For example, many words ending in -ash tend to have violent connotations (crash, smash, thrash, lash, and so on), while many of those beginning with sl- tend to have sleazy connotations (slob, slither, slime, sly, slum, and so on). Some of these sound-meaning associations seem to have an onomatopoeic source, as with the -ash words, while others are much vaguer, as with the sl- words. It is also essential to point out that within each family there are exceptions (cash, sash; sleep, slipper).

In this activity, readers of any level of ability can use simple matrices to generate nonsense words, then by reflecting on the sound qualities of the words created, they can assign meanings to the new words and use them in various contexts.

Preparation
Read through photocopiable page 119 and see whether or not you agree with the suggested connotations for the sound families listed there. Select a family and try making a sentence or two combining as many of these alliterating or rhyming words as you can, and reflect on the aesthetic qualities of your composition. Create some new words using the matrices on photocopiable 119, and repeat the exercise. Make copies of photocopiable page 119, one for each child. Make an enlarged copy of the sheet for use with the whole class.

Resources needed
Photocopiable page 119, board/flip chart.

What to do
Introduction
Show the group the word families on your enlarged copy of photocopiable page 119 and read them together using shared reading. Ask the children if they can sense any similarities in meanings between the words in each family. Write down responses and discuss them, paying particular attention to any differences of opinion. Ask the children whether there are any exceptions to the connections suggested by the given words, and point out such exceptions if the children cannot think of any.

Development
Hand out copies of photocopiable page 119 and show the children how to use the permutation matrices. After you have created a few new words by demonstrating the combination of onsets and rimes, ask the children to discuss the sounds of these words and to try to invent a meaning for them. Share your own creations and your reflections on them with the children. As the children talk, write out selected responses and help the children to work towards using these words in rhyme patterns, tongue-twisters and demonstrative sentences.

Conclusion
Ask the children to share the work they have been doing with the rest of the class. Encourage the children to think about the use of this type of language in literature, song lyrics and advertising.

Suggestion(s) for extension
More fluent readers can work with matrices which contain less frequent onsets and rimes (see the final example on photocopiable page 119). They can also write formal definitions for their new words, modelling them on the definitions that they find in different grades of school or adult dictionaries. These definitions might include specification of the part of speech of the new word, example sentences to demonstrate meaning, and even notes on the imaginary origins of the word.

Suggestion(s) for support
Instead of using a matrix, less able readers can combine onsets and rimes using a talking word processor. Type out the onsets and rimes in two columns, using 18/24 font in bold. The children, working in pairs or trios, can then use the drag and drop or cut and paste commands to combine them. The talk command can then be used to 'tell' the children what they have created. Once one set of combinations has been created by the children and recited by the computer, the group can then separate and recombine the onsets and rimes in different configurations.

Alternatively, an enlarged matrix can be completed through shared writing.

A promising way of contextualizing what might threaten to be a rather soulless exercise in generating nonsense is to use the combinations of syllables that are produced as onomatopoeic names for characters, or as choruses for songs.

Assessment opportunities
Note struggling readers' familiarity with common onsets and rimes and their ability to blend them in order to pronounce syllables. For more fluent readers, this activity provides an opportunity to assess the children's sensitivity to sound qualities.

Display ideas
Extracts from an illustrated dictionary of new words invented by the children can be displayed as a wall chart.

Other aspects of the English PoS covered
Speaking and listening: 1a, b, c; 2a, b; 3b.
Writing: 1a, b, c; 2a, d, e; 3c.

Reference to photocopiable sheet
Photocopiable page 119 provides a list of suggested connotations for various sound families. It also gives a set of permutation matrices. The children use these to create their own words.

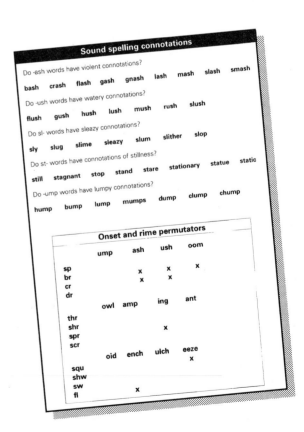

Media and miscellaneous

This chapter represents an attempt to help readers to appreciate and analyse the wealth of ambient texts that cannot be neatly categorized into discrete genres. Most adults interact with such texts on a daily basis. Some of them, like newspaper horoscopes and small ads, are ephemeral and relatively trivial; others, such as official letters, are more significant. But all of them have underlying structures which can be discussed and made explicit in order to raise readers' awareness of the textual features by which writers attempt to capture their attention and perhaps influence their behaviour. Many of these activities extend the wordplay element introduced in the previous chapter, but all of them have the ultimately serious objective of making young readers more knowledgeable about the types of texts that are directed at them, and more competent in evaluating and, when necessary, creating such texts.

A LETTER TO THE COUNCIL

To consider the issues involved in communications between the public and official bodies. To consider letters written in order to complain. To understand the appropriateness of formal/informal style.

†† *Whole class and group work follow-up.*

🕐 *20–30 minutes introduction with open-ended follow-up.*

Previous skills/knowledge needed
The activity is best done when an appropriate issue emerges in the children's own lives.

Key background information
An important aspect of reading and writing in an effective democracy is the ability of the public to read critically information relating to their lives, to make their views known to appropriate authorities, and to challenge any responses that they achieve. This activity is aimed at raising children's awareness of these issues and to consider and understand the purpose of the letter and how this affects style.

Preparation
Keep the children aware of any local issues affecting their schools or homes. A good way of doing this is to maintain a display of cuttings from the local press which children can contribute to. Higlight an issue that you feel the children may wish to pursue. Make copies of photocopiable pages 120 and 121. Enlarge them for shared reading.

Resources needed
Display as described in 'Preparation', photocopiable pages 120 and 121, local press extracts, writing materials.

What to do
Introduction
Show the children the enlarged copy of the letter to the council and discuss it in the light of the real issue which you wish to address. Help the children to evaluate the letter in terms of:
▲ its formal structure (official letter writing conventions)
▲ its relevance (stating the precise issues)
▲ its conciseness and clarity (sticking to the issues)
▲ its politeness.

Invite the children to suggest ideas for writing their own shared letter, identifying an appropriate recipient and making notes on the issues to be addressed. Compose the letter through shared writing. Demonstrate the formalities of letter writing and points about relevance, clarity and economy in the course of composition.

Development
Show the children the two replies on photocopiable page 121 and discuss their content, inviting speculation as to why the first response is so brief. Turn to the second letter and subject it to the same evaluation criteria as photocopiable page 120. Encourage the children to discuss the issues raised by the tone and content of the letter. Pay particular attention to the implied attitude of the writer. What can you infer about the writer's beliefs from what he has written? (You may like to drop a hint about condescension.)

Conclusion
Summarize your discussion and draw on this summary in order to draft a reply to Mr Seize's letter. Bear these points in mind when composing your own letters and responses.

Suggestion(s) for extension

Encourage writers to think of other people and agencies to whom they might write regarding an issue they feel strongly about. Conduct an analysis of the letters to the local press using the criteria introduced in this session.

Suggestion(s) for support

Suggest an immediate topic of controversy to the group (for example, should personal stereos for children be banned on health grounds?) and help the children to share-write a letter to an appropriate authority, stating an opinion and asking for further information. Check the first draft using the suggested criteria in the main activity, and evaluate any responses that are received in the same way.

Assessment opportunities

Note the children's mastery of letter writing conventions and their skill in stating opinions. Note also their ability to evaluate responses, paying particular attention to implied attitudes.

Opportunities for IT

The children could use a word processor to write their letter. They should not worry too much about the formatting of the letter to start with, but concentrate on the style and content of their writing. Using the word processor in this way will enable the children to go back and re-draft their letter, not just the capital letters and punctuation but the order and style of their writing.

Once they have completed the letter they can then discuss how it should be laid out and formatted. This is a good time to demonstrate to the children right alignment, in order to line up the sender's address, and full justification to even out the ragged right hand margin. It is important that children learn how to use the formatting commands such as justification, centre and the tab key rather than just using the space bar to move text to the desired position.

Display ideas

Letters and responses can be added to the display gathered together to stimulate discussion, with key points highlighted and annotated.

Other aspects of the English PoS covered

Speaking and listening: 1a, b, c; 2a, b; 3a.
Writing: 1a, b; 2a, b, c; 3a, b.

Reference to photocopiable sheets

Photocopiable page 120 contains a letter written from a concerned pupil about a proposed redevelopment on the site of an allotment. Photocopiable page 121 contains two types of reply. The children analyse all the letters according to various criteria.

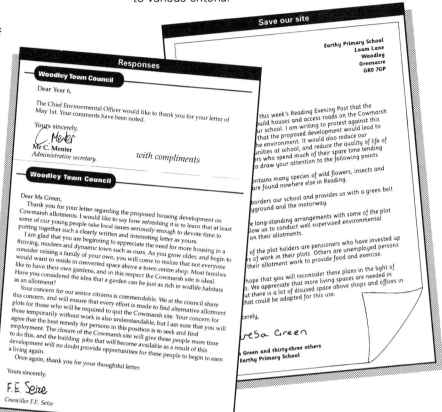

SCRAMBLE

To recognize vocabulary and discourse choices which characterize different types of newspaper. To reflect on how this affects the conveyance of news and what it implies about newspapers' beliefs about their readers.

†† *Whole class or group, including pair work.*

🕐 *20–30 minutes.*

Key background information

One of the most obvious things about newspapers is that they differ from each other vividly in the way they present information. Compare the shape and size of newspapers, the font sizes of headlines, the density of text, the proportion of the page given to pictures, the complexity and formality of language. By subjecting these differences to analysis and discussion we can raise children's awareness of the devices that are used to capture and perhaps exclude particular readerships.

Shared reading could be carried out during the first 15 minutes of the Literacy Hour, with follow-up work in the group time.

Preparation

Working with the children, make a display of a story as told in different newspapers. Make comparisons between different treatments of the same story. Draw the children's attention to factors such as the vocabulary and sentence structures used by the different papers. Cut out and mount the most vivid or off-beat stories, and invite the children to invent categories for sorting and display. Make copies of photocopiable page 122. Also make an enlarged copy for shared reading. The first example on the sheet is more challenging than the second one. For the support activity, you may like to prepare your own text based on an interest of the children's.

Resources needed

Display materials, photocopiable page 122, writing materials. For the support activity – a text based on the children's interests.

What to do

Introduction

Summarize your discussions so far of the differences between the stories on display, then present the class or group with your enlarged version of photocopiable page 122. Conduct a shared reading of the first example on the sheet, and ensure that the children have understood the basic outline of the story. Ask them to spot any obvious anomalies, for example the reference to the 'wacky prof'. You may also like to look at the reference to physical attributes and the nickname of the protagonist, as well as the use of slangy vocabulary and direct, sarcastic criticism. All these can be compared with formality and 'objectivity'.

Ask the children in which type of newspaper the story might have appeared. Steer them towards a realization that the text is a mish-mash of two different styles – formal and informal – tabloid versus broadsheet.

Development

Ask the children to work in pairs and distribute copies of the photocopiable sheet. Ask the children to identify each sentence in the examples as either formal, informal or indeterminate, providing reasons for their decisions based on observations about vocabulary and style features such as humour.

Conclusion

Pairs of children should compare their decisions about the stories. Ask them what might motivate a particular way of approaching a story: Who might the journalist be appealing to? Who might be put off by a particular style?

Suggestion(s) for extension

The issues raised by this activity can be pursued in more depth during a longer project on the media. They can also be extended to a comparison between news broadcasts of the same event on different televison channels.

Suggestion(s) for support

Conduct the entire activity through shared reading and discussion. With struggling readers it might be more useful to use the second example given on the photocopiable sheet or a story related directly to an immediate interest and to make up your own scramble. It is also useful to write the sentences out separately on long strips of paper so that an entire sentence occupies one line.

Assessment opportunities

Note the children's awareness of vocabulary choices and stylistic features, and what this implies about media perceptions of the public.

Display ideas

The children's annotations to the photocopiable sheet can be added to the display that was gathered together to stimulate this discussion.

Other aspects of the English PoS covered

Speaking and listening: 1a, b, c; 2a, b; 3a, b.
Writing: 1a, b; 2a; 3a.

Reference to photocopiable sheet

Photocopiable page 122 provides two media stories. However, both of the stories are written in a combination of styles. The children have to consider anomalies in the texts and how the different styles convey the information of the stories.

NEWSPAPERS NOW AND THEN

To investigate the language of reporting and how it has changed through time.

†† *Whole class.*

🕐 *30–40 minutes.*

Previous skills/knowledge needed

Prior to this activity you may find it useful to conduct some of the newspaper analysis activities from *Curriculum Bank Reading, Key Stage Two*, for example 'The anatomy of newspapers' on page 108, 'Matching headlines' on page 110, 'Generating headlines' on page 111, 'Exploring newspaper articles' on page 112 and 'It's a well-known fact' on page 114.

Key background information

Language change is a phenomenon that is obvious to adults but less so to children, since they have had less time to observe it happening. This activity looks at a vivid example in changes of written language. It would be a useful component of a topic on the media or history.

Shared reading could be carried out during the first 15 minutes of the Literacy Hour, with follow-up in group time.

Preparation

Scour through attics and stockrooms and make a collection of newspapers from as wide a historical period as you can. Enlist the children's help in obtaining newspapers published on their birthdate (search in your public library archives for local papers) and the antique reprints sometimes included as supplements in the more longstanding newspapers. Make a display with these, incorporating enlarged extracts and questions to draw the children's attention to differences in style and content. Make copies of photocopiable page 123, one for each child. Also make an enlarged copy for shared reading.

Resources needed

Newspaper display as described in 'Preparation', photocopiable page 123, writing materials, highlighter pens, board/flip chart.

What to do

Introduction

Summarize some of the points you have explored in the course of compiling your collection (and if you have carried out the activities in *Curriculum Bank Reading, Key Stage Two*). Tell the children that they are going to look in detail at two accounts of a shipwreck, one adapted from a turn of the century newspaper, and one showing how the story might be written now. Using your enlarged copy, conduct a shared reading of the two extracts, and allow the children five or ten minutes to share immediate reactions.

Development

Distribute individual copies of the photocopiable sheet and writing paper and ask the children to identify as many differences as they can. In particular they should look at:
▲ perspectives included in one account but omitted in the other, such as the eyewitness account of the skipper;
▲ use of eyewitness reports;
▲ choice of vocabulary and sentence structure;
▲ length of sentences.

The children should use highlighter pens and make annotations directly onto the page. They should then write a brief summary of the differences and similarities that they have found.

Conclusion

Bring the whole class back together in order to compare annotations and to share summaries. Draw a two-column chart on the board in order to record the similarities and differences. Encourage the children to think about why styles of journalism and other types of writing have changed. Has people's speech changed? You may like to compare the length of the sentences; vernacular versus literary vocabulary and the use of quoted direct speech. What kind of people become journalists now and then? Has the readership of newspapers changed? Relate this work to any activities that the children have done in comparing contemporary newspapers.

Suggestion(s) for extension

This type of comparative analysis can be extended to other types of literature from the same period, particularly children's books, for example comparing *Treasure Island* with a contemporary adventure.

Suggestion(s) for support

Divide the texts up into separate sentences, and look for ways in which parallel events have been expressed. The headline is the most obvious point of comparison.

Assessment opportunities

Note the children's sensitivity towards stylistic choices and their awareness of language change.

Display ideas

This activity lends itself to a display, as suggested in the 'Preparation' section.

Other aspects of the English PoS covered

Speaking and listening: 1a, b, c; 2a, b; 3a, b.
Writing: 1a, b.

Reference to photocopiable sheet

Photocopiable page 123 gives two newspaper reports on the same event. However, one newspaper report is from the turn of the century and the other one is contemporary. The children analyse each of the reports and the way in which they reflect language change and the nature of reporting.

TEXT COMPARISON

To explore the different perspectives on a topic that readers can gain through reading a variety of texts.

†† *Whole class.*

🕐 *30–40 minutes.*

Key background information

Literacy provides many different ways of learning about life. At a mundane level, if you want to know how to get from one place to another on a particular day, knowing how to read a transport timetable is handy. On a more general level, it is often claimed that reading good fiction can give us insights into human nature. This short activity provides a simple introduction to this idea, inviting children to think about what might be gained from reading a variety of texts.

Preparation

Nominate three or four themes that are likely to be of interest to the class (for example, a particular sport; a popular writer or singer; a current issue). Invite the children to choose one of the themes (or alternatively different pairs or groups could choose their own topic) and to contribute information from as wide a variety of texts as they can find. Make these into a display and use it as a stimulus for discussing the content and structure of the texts and what can be gained from each of them. Make an enlarged copy of photocopiable page 124.

Resources needed

Text display as described in 'Preparation', photocopiable page 124.

What to do

Introduction

Summarize your discussions on the text display and explain that you will be looking in detail at three short texts on a specific subject. Ask the children to brainstorm what they already know about hummingbirds. Make a list of the points that they come up with, then ask them to brainstorm questions. For example, curiosity questions may arise – How big do they grow? How do they hum? What do they eat? Write these down also.

Development

Show the children your enlarged copy of photocopiable page 124 and conduct a shared reading. Encourage the children to discuss the texts. How do they relate to their statements about current knowledge and their questions? Where might the texts have come from, what has been learned from them, and why were they written? This should help the readers to understand that different types of information can be gained from different genres of text, which in turn are products of different types of experience and authorial intention.

Conclusion

Redirect the children's attention to the displays that they have made on chosen topics, and ask them how the range of texts might be widened to include the type of texts that they have just examined, for example they could look for poems or autobiographical writing on a given topic.

Suggestion(s) for extension

The children can be asked to produce an exhaustive list of all the different types of documents that they should consult if they wanted to write an historical study of, for example, the local football team or a local church.

Suggestion(s) for support

Choose a popular topic such as horses or football. Find a poem, a story, an encyclopaedia entry, a newspaper article, a dictionary definition, a piece of autobiography, a song about the topic. Children can help you to collect these. Talk through what each item conveys, and how they differ.

Assessment opportunities

Note the children's awareness of likely authorship and intended readership, and the potential for learning offered by different types of text.

Opportunities for IT

The children could use a CD-ROM encyclopaedia or the Internet to research information on the different topics, noting the style and format of the information obtained from these sources. They will need to know how to print out the specific references or pages from either of these resources.

Display ideas

The text display described at the beginning of the activity can be changed and added to over a period of time.

Other aspects of the English PoS covered

Speaking and listening: 1a, b, c; 2a, b.

Reference to photocopiable sheet

Photocopiable page 124 provides different pieces of text about the hummingbird. The children read these and consider the different perspectives that can be offered on a topic.

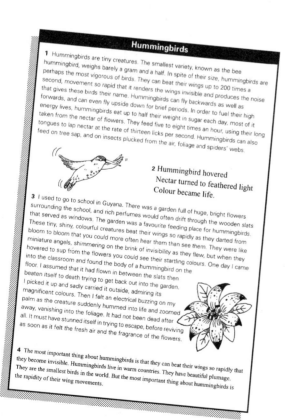

Hummingbirds

1 Hummingbirds are tiny creatures. The smallest variety, known as the bee hummingbird, weighs barely a gram and a half. In spite of their size, hummingbirds are perhaps the most vigorous of birds. They can beat their wings up to 200 times a second, movement so rapid that it renders the wings invisible and produces the noise that gives these birds their name. Hummingbirds can fly backwards as well as forwards, and can even fly upside down for brief periods. In order to fuel their high energy lives, hummingbirds eat up to half their weight in sugar each day, most of it taken from the nectar of flowers. They feed five to eight times an hour, using their long tongues to lap nectar at the rate of thirteen licks per second. Hummingbirds can also feed on tree sap, and on insects plucked from the air, foliage and spiders' webs.

2 Hummingbird hovered
Nectar turned to feathered light
Colour became life.

3 I used to go to school in Guyana. There was a garden full of huge, bright flowers surrounding the school, and rich perfumes would often drift through the wooden slats that served as windows. The garden was a favourite feeding place for hummingbirds. These tiny, shiny, colourful creatures beat their wings so rapidly as they darted from bloom to bloom that you could more often hear them than see them. They were like miniature angels, shimmering on the brink of invisibility as they flew, but when they hovered to sup from the flowers you could see their startling colours. One day I came into the classroom and found the body of a hummingbird on the floor. I assumed that it had flown in between the slats then beaten itself to death trying to get back out into the garden. I picked it up and sadly carried it outside, admiring its magnificent colours. Then I felt an electrical buzzing on my palm as the creature suddenly hummed into life and zoomed away, vanishing into the foliage. It had not been dead after all. It must have stunned itself in trying to escape, before reviving as soon as it felt the fresh air and the fragrance of the flowers.

4 The most important thing about hummingbirds is that they can beat their wings so rapidly that they become invisible. Hummingbirds live in warm countries. They have beautiful plumage. They are the smallest birds in the world. But the most important thing about hummingbirds is the rapidity of their wing movements.

To heighten children's awareness of the registers or text conventions that shape particular genres, and to explore the consequences of departing from these conventions.

✝✝ *Whole class.*

🕐 *20 minutes.*

Key background information

Register is a technical term relating to the textual features which characterize different genres or types of text. Formal legal language, for example, is very different from the language of a tabloid editorial. This activity introduces this concept at a simple level by using examples from familiar media.

Preparation

Make a display of advertisements, horoscopes, puzzle pages and competitions from popular media such as magazines, newspapers and junk mail. Ensure that you have some air freshener and toothpaste advertisements included in the display so that the children can compare them with the ones on the photocopiable sheet. Draw the children's attention to common features of these text types, such as typography, typical vocabulary, ways of addressing the reader. Make copies of photocopiable pages 125–126, one of each for each pair.

Resources needed

Display materials, photocopiable pages 125–126.

What to do

Introduction

Summarize your discussions of the display by asking the children to focus on three questions related to each category.

▲ For whom was this written?

▲ What was the author's intention?

▲ What has the author done in order to fulfil this intention?

Development

Distribute the copies of photocopiable page 125 and ask the children to compare these with one of the authentic horoscopes. They should be able to identify which four of the 'predictions' could not serve as an entry in a genuine horoscope. Ask them to specify why this is so. (One is threatening, one too specific, one insulting and one admits the futility of astrology.)

Now give out photocopiable page 126 and ask the children to compare it with genuine air freshener and toothpaste advertisements. What rules are the advertisements on the photocopiable sheet breaking? Refer back to the points discussed in 'Preparation' – the conventions of vocabulary and address.

Conclusion

Ask the children to specify the rules that have been broken by the three items that they have read. What do these rules imply about the relationship between the reader and the writer? How important is it for readers to be explicitly aware of these rules? Would it be possible to write adverts and other texts without such rules? Ask the pupils whether these items could ever serve as genuine advertisements or horoscopes. What would be the consequences?

Suggestion(s) for extension

The discussion can be related back to the work done on patterns and expectations in other forms of literature (for example, the triumph of good over evil in fairytales; the happy ending in traditional romantic fiction) and how writers can create effects by thwarting the reader's expectations. A good demonstration of this is the famous 'antilimerick':

There once was a young man from Cork
Who was stung on the arm by a wasp
When asked 'did it hurt?'
He said 'no not at all;
It can do it again if it likes.'

Suggestion(s) for support

Precede the activity with role-play in which children imitate rule-governed types of discourse, then contrast this performance with one in which the rules are broken. For example, the headteacher presenting a formal address to parents, then repeating the address in the style of a television chat show presenter; a weather presentation in the style of a funeral oration.

Assessment opportunities

Assess the children's awareness of the unstated rules governing media texts.

Display ideas

Display examples of rule-breaking discourse (ones the children may have written) alongside real-life examples of rule governed discourse. Ask the children to highlight points at which the rules have been broken.

Other aspects of the English PoS covered

Speaking and listening: 1a, b, c, d; 2a, b; 3a, b.

Reference to photocopiable sheets

Photocopiable page 125 provides an example of a horoscope but with four predictions that are not genuine. Photocopiable page 126 provides examples of two types of fake advertisements. The children have to study each of these and analyse the ways in which the register has been broken.

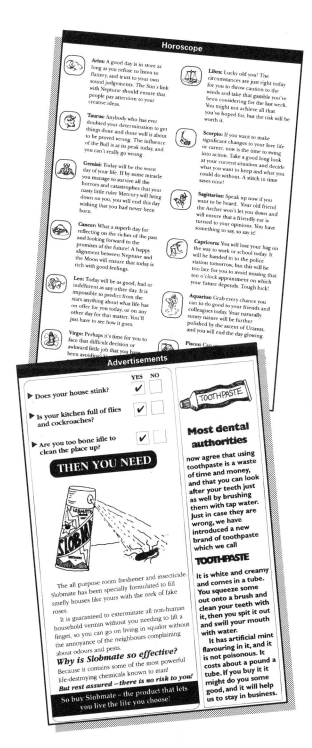

CARDS, LISTS AND POST-ITS

To investigate the conventions underlying everyday written messages.

♦♦ *Whole class.*

🕐 *Open-ended investigation.*

Key background information

Everyday engagement in literacy is less to do with reading 'literature' than reading, creating and responding to ephemeral and spontaneous texts such as lists, notes and cards. This activity is designed to raise children's awareness of the role of literacy in everyday life.

Preparation

Make as varied a collection as you can of cards that contain written messages. Save up all your lists and notes for a week and add these to the collection.

Resources needed

Collection as specified in 'Preparation', display materials, writing materials.

What to do

Discuss with the children the collection that you have gathered together and invite them to extend it. This might include any of the following items:

▲ Greetings: Christmas, Diwali, birthday, Valentines, and so on

▲ Get Well Soon and Sympathy cards

▲ Congratulations

▲ Invitations

▲ Business cards

▲ Instruction cards

▲ Recipe cards

▲ Card collections from tea and cereal packets

▲ Holiday postcards

▲ Membership cards

▲ Shopping lists

▲ Equipment lists for lessons

▲ To-do lists

▲ Lists of names of pupils to deal with

▲ Notes to self and others.

Get the children to sort these items into categories based on function, such as personal communication, notes for getting jobs done, records of experience. Select a category that is most likely to be familiar to the children. Holiday postcards would provide a good starting point. Stress the fact that though the messages to be found on the postcards will vary there are certain features that most of them will share, for example 'lightweight communication', vernacular vocabulary, mixture of tenses. Try to identify these features by encouraging the children to make up a couple of typical postcard messages, perhaps suggesting enjoyable and not so enjoyable holidays. For example:

Having a glorious time. Weather not so wonderful but improving. Spending a lot of time in interesting little shops and museums. Tomorrow we move on to the other side of the bay.
Yours....

Having a miserable time. Weather too hot to go out in. Hotel full of funny smells and cockroaches. Can't wait to get back home.
Yours....

Discuss the distinctive features of the messages that have been written, and of similar brief messages such as those on memos and greetings cards. You could point out, using such terminology as seems appropriate for your pupils, features such as the tense that is used, the type of words that are omitted and included, and the typical vocabulary of each genre.

Suggestion(s) for extension

As a longer term project, a group of children could set up a matrix or spreadsheet tabulating the type of information that the class has gathered. For example:

Type	Producer	Receiver	Printed/written	Example of text
Birthday card	friend or relative	friend or relative	both: printed poem, written message	A happy day Is coming your way Love from Mum
Recipe cards	publisher	cook	printed	Ingredients 1 egg 1 cup flour 1 pt milk

Suggestion(s) for support

Engage the children in the actual production of cards, lists and memos for practical use on a variety of occasions. Encourage them to specify the intended audience and purpose in order to make decisions about the appropriate words that need to be used.

Assessment opportunities

Note the children's awareness of purpose and audience, and how this affects content and organization of writing.

Opportunities for IT

The children could also be introduced to e-mail in this activity. Examples of e-mails could be included within the collection and the style and purpose of them included within discussions. If the school has access to e-mail and has links with other schools children could write and send their own messages.

Display ideas

The children's own messages that they produce during this activity can be displayed alongside those gathered to stimulate discussion at the start of the activity.

Other aspects of the English PoS covered

Speaking and listening: 1a, b, c; 2a, b; 3a, b.

INTERNATIONAL COMMUNICATION

To explore some possibilities for extending literacy afforded by the Internet and e-mail. To read and write in electronic media. To write to new audiences. To expand the range of texts read. To compare vocabulary and discourse styles.

†† *Whole class.*

🕐 *Open-ended.*

Key background information

The possibilities for extending literacy via the Internet and e-mail are vast and possibly limitless, but so are the opportunities for wasting time. This activity provides ideas for a focused project which uses communication technology to inspire ideas for a variety of reading and writing opportunities. It must be stressed that all Internet contacts between children and adults must be monitored.

Preparation

Talk to the children about the origin of the place name of the community in which they live, and show them how to use reference sources in order to trace the origins of this name. Ask them if they know of any other places in different countries which share the name. If they don't know, set them the challenge of finding out. Meanwhile, enter the place name into a search engine such as *Alta Vista* or *Excite*, and see what emerges. You will probably find references to same name communities in the USA or other parts of the English-speaking world. By refining your search you should be able to locate contact addresses for local bodies such as town councils and chambers of commerce. An initial enquiry should enable to you to test the feasibility of making links between your own school and one in a same name community on another continent.

Resources needed

Internet access, atlases and other reference materials, writing materials.

What to do

Explain the project to the whole class: that you want them to make contact with a community which shares the same place name, and organize the children into groups to take responsibility for the following tasks.

▲ Initial search to identify a range of possible contacts.

▲ Advanced search to narrow the options down to one or two possibilities.

▲ Making the first contact with the selected communities or schools.

▲ If the contact is successful, researching the location and other aspects of the same name community using resources such as atlases, encyclopaedias and the Internet.

▲ Drafting information about your own school and community to send to the contact school.

Suggestion(s) for extension

If the contact is successful, the opportunities for extension are practically limitless. Some possibilities for fluent readers and writers are listed below:

▲ Exchanging personal letters with children of the same age.

▲ Researching contemporary similarities and differences between the two communities.

▲ Comparative local history, including further place-name study.

▲ Exchanges of 'realia' such as newspapers, local maps and guides.

▲ Shared writing projects in genres such as autobiography and locally based fiction.

Suggestion(s) for support

Drafting concise messages about familiar events that occur in daily life for an audience which is unfamiliar with such events provides a potentially powerful motivation for reluctant readers and writers to engage in writing. Receiving a response provides a source of reading material which is likely to have a lot of personal relevance.

Assessment opportunities

Trying to assess individual children on the evidence provided by a whole-class, long-term episodic project is unlikely to be worth the effort in terms of specific, individual information.

Display ideas

The target community can be identified on a series of maps, each one 'zooming in' as the scale increases. These can all be accompanied by other graphic and written material.

Other aspects of the English PoS covered

Speaking and listening: 1a, b, c; 2a, b; 3a, b.
Writing: 1a, b, c; 2a; 3a.

WORDPLAY COMPENDIUM

To arouse curiosity about word games, and to persuade children to engage in games at word, sentence and text level in order to enhance reading and writing skills.

†† *Whole class.*

🕒 *Open-ended.*

Key background information

The tendency to play with language appears to be a universal one, and it has been estimated that more than 50 per cent of the games that feature in the pages of the print media and on television and radio involve the manipulation of words and other aspects of language. As stated in chapter three, authorities such as David Crystal (*Language Play*, Penguin) have suggested that playing with language might provide linguistic insights and flexibility that can help with the development of reading and writing skills. This activity introduces children to a variety of such games in an attempt to enthuse them into discovering and participating in more.

Preparation

Make a collection of word games from as wide a source of media as you can. Newspapers and magazines are good sources, and there are many specialized publications that consist entirely of such games. Try to pitch the games at a level which is likely to appeal to the children you teach. Display the games, together with enlarged portions of photocopiable page 127. If possible try to obtain a copy of *Language Play* by David Crystal and *The Cat's Elbow and Other Secret Languages* by Schwartz for the extension activity.

Resources needed

Display materials, photocopiable page 127.

What to do

This is an open-ended investigation which can be launched by conducting a discussion of the word games that children play spontaneously (such as the type of secret languages explored by Schwartz in *The Cat's Elbow and Other Secret Languages* Toronto: Farrar, Straus and Giroux: examples are given on the photocopiable sheet) and those that they are accustomed to from their reading and television viewing. Dedicate a regular amount of time every week to playing such games with the whole class, but try to organize time when children can engage in games without your direct supervision. Providing a bank of challenging activities, such as those exemplified on the photocopiable sheet, for the children to turn to at odd times of day, may encourage them to incorporate such games into their own play.

Suggestion(s) for extension

Language games can be extended to any level of complexity. For some ideas on possibilities for school, see the books by Schwartz and Crystal referred to above. (Crystal's book has an excellent bibliography about sources of language play.) Other books you may like to refer to include *Making the Alphabet Dance* by Ross Eckler (St. Martin's Press) and *Playing Word Games* by John Smyth (Random House).

Suggestion(s) for support

Circle games for oral language play provide a good foundation for self directed games which are more literacy oriented. Some suggestions include:

▲ Alphabetic listing games. (In my grandfather's attic I found an apple, a bible, some chalk, a dagger... each person adding another item after reciting the accumulated list.)

▲ Semantic association games (tennis, elbow, foot, mouth, talk, speak... each person responding to the last word with one related semantically).

▲ Phonological association games (speak, spider, spin, din, pin, pun, bun, fun, free... each person adding a word that rhymes or alliterates with the previous one).

▲ Sentence stretching. (Anne whispered. Last night Anne whispered. Last night Anne whispered endlessly... each person adding a word, phrase or clause to expand the sentence.)

▲ Story building (I got a shock when I went home last night... each person adds a sentence, contingent upon the sentences that have gone before.)

Assessment opportunities

This type of activity is essentially playful. Making assessment judgements would be unreliable and irrelevant.

Display ideas

This activity lends itself to many display opportunities.

Other aspects of the English PoS covered

Speaking and listening: 1a, b, c, d; 2a, b; 3a, b.
Writing: 1a, b, c; 2a, b; 3a, b.

Reference to photocopiable sheet

Photocopiable page 127 provides a number of examples of wordplay activities that can be given to the children to stimulate their play.

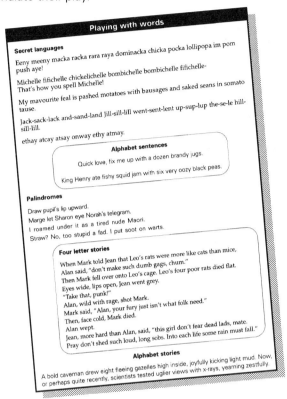

CREATING CLEAR INSTRUCTIONS

To extract key information from an extended text.
To recast information using the conventions of instructional text.

†† *Small group and pairs.*
🕐 *20–30 minutes.*

Key background information

Instructional text is characterized by economy of language and clarity of style. Only essential words are used and the instructions themselves have to be correctly ordered and succinctly expressed. In this activity, readers have to distil essential information from an extended text and use it to formulate a set of concise instructions. The skills required for this process are similar to those used in note-making and precis. This can be done during the group-work time of the Literacy Hour, or outside it as part of a practical activity.

Preparation

Collect two or three pairs of texts in which the same information is provided in an extended version and a concise version; for example a transcript of an oral account of how to get from Euston to the Millennium Dome compared with a bus and tube timetable; an explanation of how to look up a word in a dictionary compared with a flow chart. Display this material with a question prompting the children to identify similarities and differences. Also make an enlarged copy of photocopiable page 128. Obtain some examples of recipe formats from food wrappers or cook books. If you have a photocopying licence, enlarge these for shared reading.

Resources needed

Texts mentioned in 'Preparation', photocopiable page 128, paper, writing materials, recipe formats.

What to do

Introduction

Draw the children's attention to the display and discuss differences in the layout and language of the pairs of texts. Explain the concept of redundancy: that in most texts we actually have more language than we strictly need for comprehension. You could illustrate this by uttering full and abbreviated forms of command:

'Terry, could you bring your reading diary to me immediately please?'

vs

'Terry – reading diary – here – now.'

The children should be able to appreciate that in certain contexts one form of language is preferable to another. Explain that the process of this session is to create an economical instructional text from a more extended one. Point out that instructions are generally brief because practical processes, in general, need to be carried out briskly and economically, In social situations, such as the reading diary episode, we need to 'pad' our instructions in order to maintain politeness.

Development

Using your enlarged copy of photocopiable page 128, conduct a shared reading of the text, then compare it with the recipe formats. Draw the children's attention to the common features of the recipes (ingredients and method). Ask the children to scan the extended text for ingredients, highlighting these and making a list of the first two or three ingredients. Move on to the method, talking through the formulation of the first two or three steps, and demonstrating the use of concise language and imperatives (for example '1. Cream the sugar into the butter' rather than 'First of all you sprinkle the sugar into the butter and mix it up into a cream'. Ask the children to discuss which version is most clear. Does economy of language always imply greater clarity?

Recap what you have done, and allow the children to work in pairs in order to complete the recipe.

Conclusion

Pairs of children should read their recipes to the rest of the group, who should listen with the aim of assessing clarity, brevity and inclusiveness. Help the children to spot omissions, ambiguities and opportunities for further conciseness.

Suggestion(s) for extension

This procedure can be extended to a range of other text types. For example, having read an historical account of how the pyramids were built, recast this as a set of instructions; rewrite the witches' brew scene from 'Macbeth' as a recipe.

Suggestion(s) for support

For beginner readers, the entire activity can be conducted as shared reading and writing, perhaps using an initial text which might be closer to the interest and experiences of the group.

Assessment opportunities

Note the children's ability to identify key information, and to use the features of instructional text effectively.

Display ideas

Completed recipes can be added to your initial display. These could perhaps be graded in order of clarity and brevity.

Other aspects of the English PoS covered

Speaking and listening: 1a, b, c; 2a, b; 3a, b.
Writing 1a, b, c; 2a, b, c, d; 3a, b.

Reference to photocopiable sheet

Photocopiable page 128 provides long-winded instructions on how to make apple crumble. The children's task is to reduce these down into essential information.

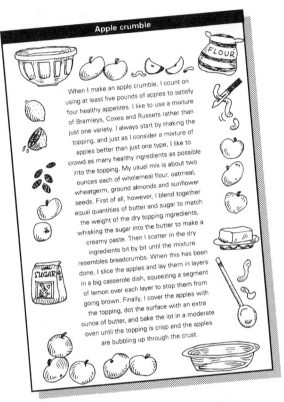

Apple crumble

When I make an apple crumble, I count on using at least five pounds of apples to satisfy four healthy appetites. I like to use a mixture of Bramleys, Coxes and Russets rather than just one variety. I always start by making the topping, and just as I consider a mixture of apples better than just one type, I like to crowd as many healthy ingredients as possible into the topping. My usual mix is about two ounces each of wholemeal flour, oatmeal, wheatgerm, ground almonds and sunflower seeds. First of all, however, I blend together equal quantities of butter and sugar to match the weight of the dry topping ingredients, whisking the sugar into the butter to make a creamy paste. Then I scatter in the dry ingredients bit by bit until the mixture resembles breadcrumbs. When this has been done, I slice the apples and lay them in layers in a big casserole dish, squeezing a segment of lemon over each layer to stop them from going brown. Finally, I cover the apples with the topping, dot the surface with an extra ounce of butter, and bake the lot in a moderate oven until the topping is crisp and the apples are bubbling up through the crust.

TEN YEARS AFTER

To encourage children to reflect on personal reading experiences and the pervasiveness of literacy in everyday life.

†† *Whole class.*

🕐 *One afternoon. This activity can provide a thought-provoking way of rounding off the school year.*

Key background information

This activity is intended to give children the opportunity to reflect on the personal significance of the reading experiences that they have had over the course of one day and one year. It might be related to time-capsule work in history. Children collect physical evidence of typical reading experiences, then file them to be untouched for ten years.

Preparation

Make a list of the most significant reading experiences you have had over the course of one year. Try not to be too precious about this. For example, reading a great,

moving poem or a letter from a long lost friend should be balanced by experiences such as reading an ingenious item of graffiti or a brochure that lead to an enjoyable holiday.

Next, make a list of all the reading experiences, significant and trivial, that you have had over the course of the last 24 hours. Try to be exhaustive, including things such as glancing at your train ticket or browsing through the small print on food packaging while waiting in a supermarket queue.

Mount a display of these lists, then the week before you do the activity, discuss the display with the class and ask them to start thinking about similar lists of their own, and making collections of the material that they have read, perhaps writing out or photocopying favourite passages from books and magazines, and making a collection of ephemera such as cards and wrappers.

In the week before you do the activity, devote an afternoon to book-making. Each child should make an A4 blank book created using a rapid method (comb binding, origami, zigzag) The books should have personalized front covers, perhaps with self portraits and should be approximately 8–16 pages long.

Resources needed
Display as described in 'Preparation', book-making materials, one zippy folder for each child, sealing wax or epoxy resin, access to photocopying facilities, writing materials.

What to do
Introduction
Tell the children about the idea of the literacy time capsule and its rationale. Explain that the time capsule could be a way of looking at current personal reading experiences, anticipating how these might change and, in say ten years time, enabling someone in the future to look back on how reading might have changed over time. You could illustrate this by citing examples of experiences such as reading e-mail or on-line encyclopaedias that for the majority of people were not available ten years ago. The experience of reading in a recently learned foreign language might also be an inspiring one.

Development
The children should paste, write or draw into their books things from their collection of material that they have read that are important to them: anything from a joke in the playground that morning, to a bus ticket, a sweet wrapper, an extract from a comic or paper, extracts from poems,

novels and information books, something that they have written, including photocopies of pieces of work they have done in other areas. On the last page of the book they write about how they are feeling right now, including their hopes and predictions for the future, and what they think they will be doing ten years from now.

Conclusion
The books are the put into see-through zippy folders, and the zips are then sealed with wax or epoxy resin. The children take them home but they must not be opened until exactly ten years have passed. Discuss with the children the pervasiveness of literacy in everyday life.

Suggestion(s) for support
Less able readers may need to be reminded of experiences that they have found enjoyable or useful. Consulting personal reading records and portfolios of written work will be helpful.

Assessment opportunities
Summative assessment of reading and writing experience is inherent in the procedures outlined above.

Opportunities for IT
It would be interesting for each child to include at least one piece of writing they have originated using a computer. The emphasis could be left to the pupils; it could be something they have written, edited, crafted or presented for a specific purpose. If the children have saved their work to disk over the year they could go back and select something done earlier.

If your school has been using e-mail or the Internet children could include some of this work; a printout of a recent e-mail, their favourite web page or part of a web page they have created themselves as part of a class project.

Display ideas
Alongside the display gathered together to stimulate discussion, the children could also display some of the items they have included in their time capsule along with reasons for their inclusion.

Other aspects of the English PoS covered
Speaking and listening: 1a, b, c; 2a, b; 3a, b.
Writing: 2e; 3a.

Deriving word meanings from context, see page 19

A walker in the storm

Many years ago a farmer was riding his horse home from the market. It was the end of a long hot summer day, and angry-looking **cumuli** were massing in the darkening **firmament**. Just as the last light **dwindled** and faded, a blinding flash of lightning lit the heavens, followed by a **colossal** clap of thunder. The rain came down in solid torrents, and before long the rider and his horse were drenched to the bones.

The farmer was not far from his village, so he carried on **steadfastly**, warily watching the stream by the side of the road which was swelling angrily as the rain filled it. He had just arrived at his farm gate when he **discerned** on the road ahead of him a young man walking alone through the cold, wet darkness, wearing only a pair of ragged and mud drenched trousers and a shirt no more **substantial** than paper.

The farmer pulled up and asked the youth who he was and where he was walking to. The youth said his name was Matthew, and that he lived in a village a mile or two further along the road. The farmer offered him **refuge** for the night, but Matthew replied that he had to get home because his mother was waiting for him.

The farmer decided to give the youth **succour**, so he helped him onto the horse and gave him a spare cloak from his saddlebag. Then he carried on riding until he arrived at the cottage where Matthew said that he lived. The farmer then realized that the youth had disappeared. He was afraid that the boy had somehow fallen off the horse during the ride home, so he knocked at the cottage door in order to get help in looking for him. A **melancholy** old woman answered the door. When the farmer told her his story, she wept and said that her only son had been dead for ten years. He had drowned after falling into a swollen stream while walking home at night through a thunderstorm.

The farmer rode home feeling **perplexed**, thinking that perhaps he had been tricked. He returned to the village the next day and visited the cemetery. There he found the grave of the youth, and over the gravestone his own cloak had been draped.

Deriving word meanings from context, see page 19

Possible meanings

Name _____   Date _____

▲ Read the story and try to work out what each word means before using a dictionary to check your ideas.

Word from the text	I think this word means	It might also mean	The dictionary says it means
cumuli			
firmament			
dwindled			
colossal			
steadfastly			
discerned			
substantial			
refuge			
succour			
melancholy			
perplexed			

Vocabulary choices in fiction, see page 21

Lexis and genre

Name _____   Date _____

▲ Fill in the missing words from the story.

Once upon a time, there lived a wise old_____who had three

_____ , each of whom was more_____than the

other two together. So_____were they that all the young

_____who lived in neighbouring lands were desperate to

_____them.

   The   loved his   , and he was anxious

that they should only_____men who were_____,

_____and_____Therefore, whenever a young

nobleman came to his_____to ask for the hand of a

_____ in marriage, the_____set the suitor a

_____to perform which could only be completed by a

_____who possessed these _____. Many

courageous young_____died in attempting to fulfil these

_____. Others lost their_____and realized that

the love of a beautiful_____was not worth the_____

to their lives.

   Eventually, the_____'s oldest _____

was married to a_____who earned

_____ hand by_____

with_____bare hands a whole

family of_____who had_____

a remote area of the kingdom for generations.

The second eldest _____ was

married to a_____who succeeded in

_____alive an immense

_____which had been haunting the

main_____of the kingdom,

swallowing _____whole

as they approached the_____.

READING KEY STAGE TWO

Vocabulary choices in fiction, see page 21

Lexis and genre (cont.)

Soon, several young _____ were in contest for the hand of
the remaining _____ . The _____
set them all a challenge.

An _____ had recently
come to _____ in the
forests on the outskirts of the kingdom,
and this _____ and
_____ creature had
_____ a whole company
of soldiers who had been sent to _____ it, chewing the
_____ from their _____ and sending their
_____ back to the castle still mounted on their terrified horses.

The _____ demanded that the first of the _____
who should return to the castle carrying the _____ of the
_____ should receive his youngest _____'s hand in
marriage as a _____ .

No sooner had the _____ set this task than the _____
made an announcement of her own.

"Father," _____ said, "spare these _____ the
danger, for I will marry none of them. I am in love with Malcolm, the _____
_____ , and I have promised him my _____ .
When we are _____ I want to _____ with him in
the _____ and help him to raise his _____ ."

The _____ was furious that his _____ had even
looked upon such a _____ young _____ let alone
fallen in love with _____ . In his anger he had the young
_____ chained up in a deep _____ in the darkest
depths of the castle dungeons, where he was left to slowly _____ .
His _____ he locked in a tiny room at the top of the castle's
highest tower, where _____ was left in _____ until
_____ should change _____ mind.

Opening paragraphs, see page 23

Opening paragraphs

Kara the Luckless

Long ago and far away, in a land of mountains and crags and caves, lived Kara the Luckless and her three beautiful daughters, Barsh, Nagrig and Ollana. One day Kara fell ill. Her daughters couldn't help her. Her doctors couldn't heal her. She knew her time was short.

Kara called her daughters to her bedside. "Soon I will die, as all mothers must," she said. "But before I die I have something to tell you. Even as I lie here a visitor is approaching whose arrival will alter the lives of all three of you. If you treat this person as I tell you, all will be well. If you treat the visitor differently, even in the smallest detail, disaster will fall upon you."

Kara gave her daughters their instructions. The visitor was not to be spoken to, nor welcomed into the house, nor allowed to see the faces of any of the three sisters. However, for each of the three nights that the visitor would call, a meal was to be prepared and left at a table that stood under an almond tree in the centre of the garden. The sisters were to take turns at preparing the meal and carrying it to the table at twilight. One by one, first Barsh, then Nagrig, then finally Ollana, the youngest daughter, promised to obey their mother's commands. Then Kara died.

How it all started

It all began on a bright summer's day when I was young and happy and everything seemed to be going my way. I was on holiday with my family. It was Saturday. I was watching the football on the TV. The sun was shining outside. My sister was playing on the beach with her friends. My parents were out shopping. I was feeling very relaxed.

Then I heard my sister calling my name. She didn't sound frightened; in fact, she sounded almost jubilantly happy, as if something was causing her an enormous amount of amusement. I could hear the excited voices of the other children, and another peculiar sound that I couldn't identify. I went out to see what was going on.

I found my sister and the other children, two boys and another girl, all aged around ten or eleven, standing around the tall white platform that the lifeguards sit on to keep watch over the beach. They were looking up and laughing in delight. I looked up as well when I reached them, but what I saw didn't delight me at all. In fact, I felt sick.

Tracking cohesive links, see page 27

A box of tricks

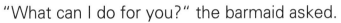

One day an old man in an old fashioned sailor's outfit walked into a pub near the docks in Liverpool and sat on a stool at the bar.

"What can I do for you?" the barmaid asked.

"I'll take a glass of rum," the old salt replied.

The man sat and sipped his drink quietly, and when he had finished it, he gave a whistle and a battered old seaman's chest came rolling into the pub on four little wheels as if it could steer itself. There was a skull and crossbones engraved on the lid, and the name *Tristram Trincomalee* on the side.

"What on earth is that?" the barmaid demanded.

"Just my old box of tricks," the strange old man replied.

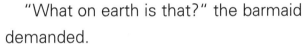

He gave another whistle, and the ancient chest opened itself up with a creak of rusty hinges. A smell of tobacco and spices and seaweed poured out of the chest, followed by the sound of booming waves and sea shanties sung to the strains of an accordion.

"What on earth do you keep in that thing?" the barmaid asked.

The old sailor winked at her.

"What on earth *don't* I keep in it?" he replied.

The poor man's dream

Name _____   Date _____

▲ Fill in the missing words from the story.

Jack lived in a cramped house with cracked windows and a leaky roof. One dying apple tree grew in the tiny, muddy garden. Jack had no work and he and his wife had to go hungry many a day.

One night Jack had a dream and woke up laughing.

"What's so funny?" said his wife. "We've nothing but stale crumbs in the larder and nothing but holes in our pockets."

"I'll tell you in the morning," said Jack.

But in the morning, Jack had forgotten his dream. All he could remember was that riches awaited him if he would go to London and stand on London Bridge. His wife thought him mad, but Jack decided to follow his dream and leave for the city.

"When I return, we will be rich," he said.

So Jack trudged the hundred miles to London and stood for seven days and seven nights on London Bridge, starving and freezing. At the end of the week he sadly gathered his rags about him and turned to leave. I might as well die at home as here, he thought. Just then, a pieman came up to Jack and offered him a few broken crusts.

"I've been watching you standing there all week," said the pieman. "What is it you're waiting for?"

"I don't know," said Jack. "I had a dream the other week, and woke up thinking that if I came to London and stood on the bridge I'd get rich."

"A dream!" the pieman laughed. "The world would be a funny place if we all followed our dreams! Why, only last night I had a ridiculous dream that

_____

_____ "

Then Jack knew exactly what he had to do. He thanked the pieman and set off on the long walk home. As soon as he arrived he

_____

_____ .

Jack and his wife lived happily ever after.

Missing pieces, see page 29

The voices of the clocks

Name _____   Date _____

▲ Fill in the missing words from the story.

Lola lived with her father and mother in a big house in the city of London. They were a very rich family and Lola was used to being given everything that she wanted.

   One day Lola was walking with a friend in London when she saw a gold watch in a jeweller's window, attached to a very long golden chain. It looked so wonderful that Lola made her mind up that she would tell her parents to buy it for her.

   When she arrived home, however, she found her parents in a bad mood. Her father had lost his job in the City. When Lola told him that she wanted the gold watch, he laughed at her. When Lola sulked, he scowled and told her to go away.

   The next day, Lola went to the jeweller's shop and stole the watch. She scurried home with it and crept up to her bedroom where she could admire it in secret. But as soon as she took it out and cupped it in her hands, she was astonished to hear a voice coming from inside it.

"_____," said the watch.

Lola was frightened. She wrapped the watch in a towel and crammed it into her bag and fled into the street before anybody in the house could hear it. She saw a big clock above the public library, and as soon as her eyes fell upon the face of the clock, a loud voice came from inside it.

"_____," said the clock.

Lola was terrified. Now everybody in the neighbourhood will know, she thought. She ran in panic down into the tube station and caught a train to Westminster. As soon as she came out of the station she saw Big Ben looking down at her, and the moment the huge clock saw her, it began to chime with a human voice.

"_____," said Big Ben.

Lola was horrified. Now everybody in London will know, she thought. There was only one thing to do. Lola hurried over to the jeweller's shop and gave the watch back. The jeweller had already called the police, and Lola was given a severe warning, but never again did she steal anything, and never again did she hear the voices of the clocks.

Anna's story

Anna lived alone in a stone hut deep in the forest. Every day she had to gather wood for the fire, draw water from the stream, and pick whatever fruits and roots she could find growing wild in the forest. She had nobody to help her and nobody to talk to.

One day Anna was on her way to the stream when she heard the sound of somebody splashing in the water, so she hid in the bushes and tried to see who it was. She saw a young man climb out of the stream. He sat on a rock and began to sing in the most beautiful voice she had ever heard. Then he unfolded a bundle that lay nearby. It was a cloak of feathers. He put it on and instantly turned into a tiny, colourful bird. Then he spread his wings and flew away.

The next day Anna hid by the stream again. In the afternoon she saw a tiny colourful bird land on the rock. The bird fluttered a little, its feathers fell away, and Anna saw the young man standing on the rock. He folded up the cloak of feathers that lay at his feet and plunged into the stream.

Anna crept out of hiding, seized the cloak of feathers, and ran home with it. She hid it in the roof of her house. Then she waited until darkness was falling and walked back to the stream. The young man was sitting on the rock, but instead of singing he was weeping pitifully, and shivering.

Anna wrapped the young man in her own cloak and took him back to her house. She tried to talk to him but he could only weep and make cooing and singing noises. She looked after the young man for a long time. Soon he stopped crying and began to trust her. After much longer he learned to speak. After much longer again he and Anna fell in love and got married.

Anna's life changed. Her husband kept her company, sang beautiful songs to her, and helped her with all the hard work. Together they planted a garden around the house and grew flowers and vegetables. They had two children who grew up to be strong and healthy. The man seemed to be happy in the forest, but very often he would start to cry when he heard the birds begin to sing in the morning, or when he saw them flying south for the winter.

One day Anna went out with her older child to collect wood. When she came home she found that her husband had gone away. Her younger child, who was crying pitifully, told Anna that his father had found a cloak of feathers when he was fixing the roof, and that he had put it on and vanished. Anna never saw her husband again, but sometimes, when she was sitting in the garden with her children, a tiny colourful bird would flutter down and watch them very sadly.

Fostering uncertainty – inferences, see page 32

Deduction and inference

Name _____   Date _____

The man who appeared by the stream came from _____

_____

but it is also possible that he came from _____

_____ .

I think that Anna stole the feather cloak because _____

_____

but she might instead have taken it because _____

_____ .

Anna went back to the river after stealing the cloak because _____

_____

but she could also have gone back because _____

_____ .

I think the man was weeping because _____

_____

but he might instead have been weeping because _____

_____ .

I think that the man could not speak because _____

_____

but another reason could be that _____

_____ .

I think that Anna's husband disappeared because _____

_____

but it is also possible that he _____

_____ .

A nice soft bed

"She's waking up."

Who said that? Not Mum's voice. Too gruff. Why'd she want to wake me anyway? Nice soft bed. Sleep a bit longer.

"I should think so too. She's got a nerve taking a snooze there!"

Someone else. Sounds a bit like Dad when he's got one of his sore throats. Bad-tempered too. What's wrong with taking a snooze in a lovely soft bed? Just a few more minutes and then I'll open my eyes and get up.

"Shall we gobble her up?"

Gobble me up? Gobble me up! What's going on here? Must be dreaming. Just roll over and think of something nice.

"She certainly deserves it after what she did downstairs. We've got to get food from somewhere to make up for the breakfasts she stole."

Breakfast? Feel as if I've had breakfast already somewhere. Yes, a nice warm bowl of porridge, not too hot, not too cold. As lovely and warm as this bed. This nice comfortable bed. Much more comfortable than those chairs I sat on.

"And she certainly doesn't deserve to be lying in my bed after smashing my chair up. What if she breaks this as well?"

       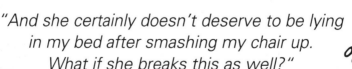   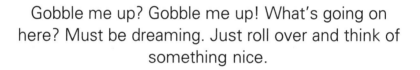

Time perspectives, see page 37

The fugitive

On a cold November morning, the day of my thirtieth birthday, I took up my pen and started to describe what had happened twenty years before when I first saw Harry Terror climbing over the garden wall of the house my parents owned near London Zoo, a knife between his teeth and a top hat on his head. A year has gone by since Harry disappeared when his ship, *The Arctic Tern*, sank without trace in a freezing ocean, and it has been ten years since I last met Harry face to face while we were both working on a Jamaican banana plantation. But I think about him often, and my strongest memory is my first one: of a lanky and long-haired young man jumping from the garden wall into my father's prize dahlias, and making his way towards the back of our house. He was a complete stranger, but there was something in the confident way he strolled through the garden that would have made you believe he owned the house I was born in. My twin sister and I had planted two apple trees in the garden on our fifth birthday, and as Harry walked between them, he paused and picked himself the handsomest apple he could reach. He used his knife to slice it in half before putting the weapon into his back pocket. Then he ambled up to our back door. I withdrew from the window in alarm and ran to the top of the stairs just in time to see my father opening the door.

"Excuse me for intruding," Harry said through a mouthful of Granny Smith, "but I've just been chased into your garden by an escaped orang-utan, and I need to phone the police."

Predicting from settings, see page 39

Locations

PARADISE GARDENS

Paradise Gardens lay between Lionheart Towers to the east and west and Churchill Court to the north. To the south, beyond the bypass, there was nothing but the ruins of the abandoned factories in which the unemployed residents of the Court and the Towers had once worked.

Nothing grew in Paradise Gardens except nettles, bindweed, unkempt sycamores and a handful of other species who find it difficult to die. The soil in the flowerbeds had solidified under a thick layer of crushed cans and junk-food wrappers. The fountain at the centre of the gardens that had once flung out sparkling streamers of water was dry now, but richly adorned with a crust of colourful spray-paint slogans.

THE WASTELAND

The last of the hunters lived at the tip of a rocky peninsula jutting into a sea that was frozen solid for nine months of the year. Winds sharp enough to strip the skin off a man swept across their camps for weeks at a time, and during the long winters the hunters could see no further than the perpetual blizzards would allow them to.

In spring, the ice crust broke up in a din of lifeless shouts and groans. The stone-hard snow shrank from the rocks and bright flowers briefly bloomed around the camp. Seals squirmed ashore to bear their pups on the little beaches that formed the floors of the chasms breaking the shoreline. The sky teamed with birds and the waters with fish.

Common plights, see page 42

What next?

Simon is one of the most cheerful children in his class at school. He does well at all his lessons. He is good at sport and is well liked because of his fairness and generosity. One day a new boy joins Simon's class.

Fabio is a shepherd who spends most of the year looking after his flocks on the mountainside. He enjoys the hard, healthy outdoor life of a shepherd. One spring morning he has to visit a market in the city. He meets a rich merchant's daughter and falls in love with her. He asks her to come with him into the mountains.

Margaret is visiting some friends who live in a different town. They take her to visit a ruined mansion house which they say is haunted. Margaret says that they are silly, because there are no such things as ghosts.

A king tells his three daughters that he has to go on a long journey. He warns them not to misbehave when he is away. In particular, they must not walk into a certain room in the cellars of the castle.

Andrea and Bianca are sisters. Andrea is kind but Bianca is rather selfish. One day they are picking blackberries in the forest when they encounter an old lady who has dropped her firewood. She asks the two girls to help her.

Lee is a weak and timid man who is despised by most of the tough guys in the frontier town in which he lives. One day the town is taken over by cruel and murderous invaders.

As a child, Ella is given a special doll by her godmother, who warns her never to neglect it. Ella looks after the doll until she is 16, then she leaves it in the cellar and forgets about it.

Genres within non-fiction, see page 46

Episode at Chernobyl

Nuclear explosions are the most destructive events ever to have occurred on Earth. They are caused by a process called nuclear fission, which occurs when the nucleus of an atom of a radioactive substance such as uranium or plutonium splits. The nucleus can be made to split by bombarding it with sub-atomic particles known as neutrons. The splitting of the atom releases a massive amount of heat energy and more neutrons, which strike neighbouring atoms, causing them to split as well, releasing yet more energy and yet more neutrons. This is known as a nuclear chain reaction, an immensely powerful process which is very difficult to control.

In an atom bomb, the chain reaction takes place in a fraction of a second, causing a vast explosion and the release of lethal radiation. In a nuclear reactor, rods of uranium or plutonium are lowered into a reactor which causes a slower chain reaction to begin. The reaction generates a huge amount of heat which is used to create steam for the generation of electricity. The speed of the reaction can be controlled by inserting into the reactor rods of a substance such as graphite, which absorbs the escaping neutrons. Lowering the control rods completely can shut the reactor down. When the control rods are lifted, the reaction speeds up. To prevent the escape of radiation, the reactor is encased in a steel shell surrounded by concrete.

During the night of Friday 24th – Saturday 25th April, 1986, a team of engineers were preparing Reactor 4 at the Chernobyl nuclear power station in the Ukraine for shutdown. This would enable them to carry out maintenance and repairs. They also hoped that when the flow of energy had decreased to a certain point, they would be able to carry out some important tests before shutdown.

Graphite control rods were inserted into the reactor core, and the flow of energy began to slow down. At about midnight, the engineers attempted to begin the tests, but they discovered that the power of the reactor was already too low. The two head engineers judged that it was now too late for the tests to take place, and that the reactor should be allowed to shut down. Their supervisor, however, was impatient for the tests to go ahead, and decided to risk a rapid restart of the reactor. He ordered that the control rods should be immediately raised.

The engineers obeyed, and a huge blast of energy surged through the system, straining the pipes and turbines which processed the steam. By 1.23am the whole system appeared to be at breaking point, and one of the engineers announced that he was going to press an emergency button that would lower all the control rods into the reactor. Had he succeeded, the power station might have been saved. But the rods jammed, and seconds later there was a vast explosion.

Formality and authority, see page 48

Miracles of nature? (1)

The elephant's trunk

If elephants ever developed a liking for a nice cup of tea every now and then, their trunks are perfectly well-adapted to pouring water from kettle to pot and tea from pot to cup. It is probable that they could even be trained to add milk and sugar!

An elephant's trunk can grow to a length of two metres and achieve a girth as thick as the thigh of a stout human being. The trunk contains 60,000 muscles, and is powerful enough to wrench trees out of the ground and to lift and manoeuvre huge logs. Yet the trunk is also astonishingly delicate. An elephant can grip a pencil in its trunk and draw on paper with it. It can pull out thorns and pick up pins. It can even uncork a bottle!

As well as being delicate, the trunk is also extremely sensitive. A blindfolded elephant can use its trunk to identify objects, and the nerve endings inside the trunk enable the elephant to smell food, or enemies, a mile or more away. So any elephant who did become a tea drinker would be able to sniff out whether or not the supermarket stocked its favourite blend without having to go in and ask!

The tardigrade

How would you feel if somebody shut you in an oven hotter than the boiling point of water, or froze you in a fridge set to a temperature of –272°C, or pressed you under a weight of several tons? I suppose that the answer must be 'nothing', because any one of these three ordeals would kill you very quickly indeed.

To a tardigrade, however, being baked, frozen and squashed like this count as minor discomforts. A tardigrade looks like a caterpillar with four pairs of clawed legs, but it is a mere fifth of a millimetre long. In spite of its minuscule size and undramatic appearance, it is probably the most indestructible creature in the world. Scientists have roasted tardigrades to temperatures as high as 150°C and as low as –272°C and they have survived. Tardigrades have been crushed under pressures twice as high as those that have been shown to kill all other animals, and they have thrived. Tardigrades have even been dried out into dust; but once they have been sprinkled into water, they have rehydrated themselves and started to wriggle about as if nothing had happened.

Some scientists think that tardigrades could exist in outer space. They are certainly tough enough to withstand any environment on Earth, not to mention the cruellest trials inflicted on them by so-called human beings.

Formality and authority, see page 48

Miracles of nature? (2)

The rat louse

This new subspecies of the genus *pediculus* acquires its popular name from both its size and its propensity to attack and eat rats. The first specimens of the rat louse were discovered ten years ago in disused warehouses near the

Windscale Nuclear Power station in Cumbria, and are thought to have resulted from genetic mutations to the common head louse. Rat lice grow up to 30 centimetres in length and can weigh more than a kilogram. They are too large to survive unnoticed as parasites on humans or other mammals, but they appear to have quickly developed alternative forms of sustenance. Initially surviving by scavenging from rubbish dumps and thieving from workers' canteens, rat lice are now thought to pose a threat to the survival of small mammals in the north of England and southern Scotland. Their similarity to discarded junk food containers when curled up enables them to ambush unsuspecting victims such as rats, hedgehogs and foxes. All of these mammals are relatively slow moving, and forage for food in urban environments, usually by night. While they are doing this, they are seized by the disguised rat louse, overpowered, and quickly drained of blood.

The bibliogar

The bibliogar is the only animal known to incorporate literature into its diet. Bibliogars are a variety of budgerigar which were specially bred by librarian and schoolteacher bird-fanciers for their quiet voices and studious manner. The unique diet of this variety of domestic bird was discovered when one of the keepers of the first generation of bibliogars noted that his bird appeared to be taking a keen interest in the newspaper which had been spread on the bottom of the cage to catch droppings. It has since been shown that on acquiring their first plumage, the birds begin to scan their surroundings for printed materials, and pine restlessly when this is not available. In contrast, young bibliogars who are surrounded by various types of print gain weight rapidly and acquire exceptionally sweet and complex voices. Bibliogars have been seen to use their beaks and wings to turn the pages of small books left in their cages, and to put these books carefully to one side once they have been thoroughly perused. Recent generations of bibliogars have displayed preferences for specific types of literature, some thriving best on poetry and romantic fiction, others on information books and computer-generated text.

Bias in information texts, see page 50

Biographies

Guevara, Ernesto 'Che' (1928–67): Argentinian communist and revolutionary. After graduating as a doctor in 1953, Guevara abandoned medicine for politics, and played a key role in the violent overthrow of the Cuban government, helping Fidel Castro to seize power and establish his dictatorship in 1959. He held government posts after the revolution, but in 1965 he left Cuba in order to spread communist doctrine in other impoverished countries. He is known to have attempted to lead an unsuccesful insurrection in central Africa before returning to South America. During an incompetent campaign against the Bolivian government, he led his troops into an ambush. Guevara was captured and executed in October 1967.

Guevara, Che (Ernesto) (1928–67): Argentinian doctor and liberation leader, given the affectionate nickname 'Che' by his admirers. Che graduated in medicine in 1953, but soon afterwards decided that he could best relieve suffering by fighting injustice rather than disease. He played a key role in the heroic struggle that overthrew the Batista dictatorship in Cuba, and afterwards assisted his friend Fidel Castro in the government of the liberated country. In 1965, however, he rejoined the struggle against tyranny, leading a brave but doomed campaign in central Africa before returning to lead a liberation movement in Bolivia. Che was captured by Bolivian forces in October 1967. In spite of being wounded, he offered to treat enemy casualties, but he was murdered by his captors and his body buried in secret.

Columbus, Christopher (1451–1506): Genoan mariner and explorer, discoverer of the New World. Columbus first went to sea at the age of 14, and survived a shipwreck in 1470. Seven years later he began to seek a patron for a bold expedition to sail westward to India: an idea which was greeted with ridicule and disbelief. Eventually he found backing from Ferdinand and Isabella of Castille, and in 1492 embarked on the journey that was to bring him to the Caribbean and the Americas. Columbus made four voyages to the New World, all of them frought with great danger and he had to cope with difficulties from travelling companions who were less bold than he was. He died in Spain and his remains lie in Seville cathedral.

Colon, Cristobal (1451–1506): Genoan merchant and adventurer who initiated the colonialization of the Caribbean and the Americas and the extermination of their original inhabitants. Colon conceived the idea that India could be reached by sailing west, and after receiving royal backing from Ferdinand and Isabella of Castille, he set off in August 1492 and reached the Caribbean in October. Colon was not a skilled mariner, and this and subsequent voyages were frought with great danger for his crew members, whom he treated very harshly. Colon's establishment of settlements in the New World directly led to the destruction of the civilizations of the original inhabitants.

Lexical cohesion in information texts, see page 53

Pumpkins

1 Pumpkins are among the most nutritious vegetables that have ever been cultivated. The flesh of a pumpkin is rich in Vitamins A, C and E, and contains a wide variety of minerals. High levels of easily digestible sugars make this an excellent source of carbohydrate. The young leaves abound in Vitamin C, fibre and iron. Pumpkin seeds are excellent sources of protein and polyunsaturated fats. Even the pumpkin flower is edible, and is as rich in nutrients as the flesh and the leaves.

2 Pumpkins are one of the most versatile vegetables in the kitchen. They can be cut into wedges and roasted in their skins with a little butter to make a tasty, sweet-flavoured golden vegetable. They can be boiled with their own weight in sugar to make a delicately flavoured jam. The flesh can be puréed with honey, nutmeg and cinnamon and used as a pie filling. The seeds can be roasted and nibbled as a snack. Even the flowers can be dipped in batter, fried and stuffed with soft cheese.

3 Pumpkins are one of the easiest crops for the inexperienced gardener to grow. For relatively little effort you can have a rapidly growing and attractive ground cover which will keep down your weeds under a carpet of attractive foliage adorned with golden trumpet-like flowers. Plant the seeds two or three to a cluster in positions at least a metre apart after the danger of frost has passed. It is advisable to plant them in a 30-centimetre cubic hole which you have stuffed with well-rotted farmyard manure. When the seed leaves open, thin to the strongest plant and water generously throughout the summer, feeding with a liquid fertilizer once a week. The fruit will begin to swell in August and will be ready for harvesting in September or October when the leaves are dying down.

Information exchange, see page 57

Interview information A

For countless generations, farmers in India and other Third World countries have kept a proportion of the seed harvested from wheat and rice crops in order to raise next year's plants from it. Traditionally, seed has been shared and exchanged without any money changing hands, so that even the poorest farmer can benefit from his own labour and that of his neighbours.

These traditional farming practices have been changing recently. Agricultural corporations who produce genetically modified seeds are advertising these seeds to Indian farmers, telling them that if they buy them, they will obtain much better crops than if they keep using their own seeds. They often offer loans to farmers so that the farmers can buy the seeds, on the understanding that they will pay the companies back when the crops have been harvested.

However, when the farmers have sown the seeds, they find the plants they produce will not grow properly without expensive chemical fertilizers. They are also more vulnerable to disease and pests, so the farmers have to buy more expensive chemicals in order to control these problems. But the worst thing about the plants is that they have been modified to produce seeds which will not grow into new plants the next season. This means that once a farmer has started to grow them, he has to buy new seeds every year, and fresh supplies of fertilizers, weedkillers and pesticides. Many of the poorest farmers have been bankrupted by these developments, and some have even killed themselves in despair.

Now farmers in India are fighting back. They have called for a ban on the sales of the new seeds, and some sites in which the corporations produce them have been burned by protesters. Perhaps there is still time to return to a more sustainable way of farming.

Information exchange, see page 57

Interview information B

Most of the bananas that you see on sale in Europe have been grown in Central America, but about eight per cent have been imported from the island nations of the Caribbean.

Central American banana farming is very different from that of the Caribbean. The banana plantations of Central America are vast. They are owned by rich international corporations who can afford to use machinery to cultivate and harvest the banana plants. These corporations pay their workers very low wages to keep the cost of bananas down. They use large amounts of pesticides and fertilizers so that the bananas are disease-free and grow to a large size.

The islands of the Caribbean are small and very mountainous, so the banana farms on these islands are tiny. They are owned by poor families who depend on the banana trade for their livelihood. These farmers cannot afford machinery, or expensive pesticides and fertilizers. They often carry their bananas by hand from the plantation to the boxing shed, and many are damaged in the process. Their bananas are therefore more expensive to produce than Central American ones, and they cost more in the shops. They tend to be smaller, but many people claim that they taste better.

Europe has been allowing Caribbean nations to sell them a guaranteed percentage of their produce, because the farmers of the Caribbean will either starve or turn to growing marijuana and cocaine if their bananas are priced out of the market. But now this arrangement is threatened by the corporations, who claim that the European guarantee is unfair and should be banned. Many people feel that Britain, which established the Caribbean banana industry when it controlled much of the region, is particularly responsible for protecting the poorer farmers.

Information exchange, see page 57

Interview questions

Interview questions A

▲ Ask your partner the following questions, and note his or her answers.

1 What main features of traditional farming practices does the writer describe?

2 What is the writer's attitude towards these practices?

3 What change or changes in practice does the writer describe?

4 What is the writer's attitude towards the change?

5 What do you think is the attitude of the new seed producers towards their customers in the Third World?

6 What might people in Europe do to alleviate the effects of the changes described in the passage?

7 Are there any statements in the passage with which you disagree?

8 What is the most interesting thing you have learned from this passage?

9 What questions would you like to ask about the subject matter of this passage?

- -

Interview questions B

▲ Ask your partner the following questions, and note his or her answers.

1 Name two differences between Caribbean bananas and those that are grown in Central America.

2 Can you think of any reasons for the alleged difference in taste between American and Caribbean bananas?

3 Why are Caribbean farmers so dependent on the banana trade?

4 Do you think that Europe is protecting the Caribbean banana trade for purely humanitarian reasons?

5 Why do you think that the rich corporations are so insistent on removing the small percentage of the market which is set aside for Caribbean bananas?

6 On the basis of what you have just read, can you think of any ways in which Europe could help the farmers of the Caribbean?

7 Are there any statements in the passage with which you disagree?

8 What is the most interesting thing you have learned from this passage?

9 What questions would you like to ask about the subject matter of this passage?

Paragraphing, see page 60

Sentence shuffle

Earthquakes and volcanoes are extremely destructive natural phenomena.

They tend to occur in particular zones of the Earth's surface.

The edges of the great plates on which continents float come together in these zones.

When the plates pull away from each other, or grind over each other, this causes powerful vibrations which are known as earth tremors.

The point from which the vibrations of an earthquake originate is known as the epicentre.

If the epicentre lies below or close to a city, it is likely that there will be extensive damage to buildings, roads, bridges and other structures.

The collapse of these structures can cause injury or loss of life.

Even when the epicentre lies outside of a city, earth tremors are likely to cause fissures in the ground, dramatic uplift and subsidence of land, and dangerous avalanches.

Even earthquakes occurring in the most remote locations can be dangerous.

When an earthquake occurs below the seabed, the disruption will cause massive displacements of water.

This will produce a powerful wave or a series of such waves which will spread out from the epicentre, often travelling at several hundred kilometres per hour.

When these waves reach shallower seas they slow down, but build up into massive walls of water.

These tidal waves or tsunamis can utterly devastate coastal communities.

What makes a poem a poem?, see page 64

Poetry and prose

Doctor Foster
Went to Gloucester
In a shower of rain
He stood in a puddle
Right up to his middle
And never went there again.

A man called Doctor Foster went to Gloucester on a rainy day. He stood in a puddle and sank right up to his middle, so he decided never to go to Gloucester again.

I wandered lonely as a cloud
That floats on high o'er vales and hills,
When all at once I saw a crowd,
A host, of golden daffodils.
Beside the lake, beneath the trees,
Fluttering and dancing in the breeze.

Continuous as the stars that shine
And twinkle on the milky way,
They stretched in never-ending line
Along the margin of a bay:
Ten thousand saw I at a glance,
Tossing their heads in sprightly dance.

The waves beside them danced; but they
Out-did the sparkling waves in glee:
A poet could not but be gay,
In such a jocund company:
I gazed - and gazed - but little thought
What wealth the show to me had brought:

For oft, when on my couch I lie
In vacant or in pensive mood,
They flash upon that inward eye
Which is the bliss of solitude;
And then my heart with pleasure fills,
And dances with the daffodils.

I was out walking on my own near a lake one day when I saw a huge swathe of about ten thousand daffodils swaying about in the breeze. They looked so cheerful that they made me feel very happy. Even now, when I'm on my own and feeling thoughtful, I remember exactly what they looked like and it really cheers me up.

White plum blossom shone
In moonlight: I thought I saw
First light of morning!

I was out in the dark one night when I saw a light in front of me. I thought it was the first light of morning but it turned out to be moonlight reflected on white plum blossom.

Mysterious poetry

from **A Child's Garden of Verses**
by Robert Louis Stevenson

Whenever the moon and stars are set,
Whenever the wind is high,
All night long in the dark and wet,
A man goes riding by.
Late in the night when the fires are out.
Why does he gallop and gallop about?

Whenever the trees are crying aloud,
And ships are tossed at sea,
By, on the highway, low and loud,
By at the gallop goes he.
By at the gallop he goes, and then
By he comes back at the gallop again.

The White Rabbit's Evidence from **Alice in Wonderland**

They told me you had been to her,
And mentioned me to him:
She gave me a good character,
But said, I could not swim.

He sent them word I had not gone
(We know it to be true):
If she should push the matter on,
What would become of you?

I gave her one, they gave him two,
You gave us three or more;
They all returned from him to you,
Though they were mine before.

If I or she should chance to be
Involved in this affair,
He trusts to you to set them free,
Exactly as we were.

My notion was that you had been
(Before she had this fit)
An obstacle that came between
Him, and ourselves, and it.

Don't let him know she liked them best,
For this must ever be
A secret, kept from all the rest,
Between yourself and me.

Metaphors

A messenger tells of Macbeth's encounter with an enemy:

...he unseam'd him from the nave to the chaps
And fixed his head upon our battlements.

Macbeth replies to the witch who has addressed him as Thane of Cawdor:

The Thane of Cawdor lives: why do you dress me
In borrowed robes?

Macbeth longs for sleep after the murder of Duncan:

Sleep that knits up the ravell'd sleave of care

Macbeth looks forward to the night in which Banquo will be murdered:

...Come, seeling night
Scarf up the tender eye of pitiful day.

Macbeth's avenging enemies approach his castle:

...now does he feel his title
Hang loose about him, like a giant's robe
Upon a dwarfish thief.

Compounds, coinages and kennings, see page 74

Compounds, coinages and kennings

Compounds
▲ Can you find some other compound words to add to this list?

anteater	newspaper
buttercup	overboard
candlestick	penfriend
dragonfly	quagmire
eggcup	railway
farmhouse	sunrise
greyhound	teacake
hedgehog	underpants
inkwell	vineyard
jamjar	woodworm
kneecap	xylophone
lighthouse	yearbook
molehill	zigzag

Compound coinages
▲ These compounds are made up words. Make up some more yourself and write definitions for them.

antworm

butterphone

candlepants

Kennings
▲ Make up some kennings of your own.

ant —— stingswarmer

bee —— honeyguts

Onset and rime onomatopoeia generators, see page 77

Sound spelling connotations

Do -ash words have violent connotations?

bash　　**crash**　　**flash**　　**gash**　　**gnash**　　**lash**　　**mash**　　**slash**　　**smash**

Do -ush words have watery connotations?

flush　　**gush**　　**hush**　　**lush**　　**mush**　　**rush**　　**slush**

Do sl- words have sleazy connotations?

sly　　**slug**　　**slime**　　**sleazy**　　**slum**　　**slither**　　**slop**

Do st- words have connotations of stillness?

still　　**stagnant**　　**stop**　　**stand**　　**stare**　　**stationary**　　**statue**　　**static**

Do -ump words have lumpy connotations?

hump　　**bump**　　**lump**　　**mumps**　　**dump**　　**clump**　　**chump**

Onset and rime permutators

	ump	ash	ush	oom
sp				
br		X	X	X
cr		X	X	
dr				

	owl	amp	ing	ant
thr				
shr				
spr			X	
scr				

	oid	ench	ulch	eeze
squ				X
shw				
sw				
fl		X		

A letter to the council, see page 79

Save our site

Earthy Primary School
Loam Lane
Woodley
Greenacre
GR0 7GP

1 May 1999

Dear Councillor,

I have read in this week's Reading Evening Post that the council has plans to build houses and access roads on the Cowmarsh allotment site near our school. I am writing to protest against this plan because I think that the proposed development would lead to serious damage to the environment. It would also reduce our educational opportunities at school, and reduce the quality of life of the allotment holders who spend much of their spare time tending their plots. I wish to draw your attention to the following points

The site contains many species of wild flowers, insects and mammals which are found nowhere else in Reading.

The site borders our school and provides us with a green belt between the playground and the motorway.

We have long-standing arrangements with some of the plot holders who allow us to conduct well supervised environmental investigations on their allotments.

Many of the plot holders are pensioners who have invested up to thirty years of work in their plots. Others are unemployed persons who rely on their allotment work to provide food and exercise.

We hope that you will reconsider these plans in the light of these points. We appreciate that more living spaces are needed in Reading, but there is a lot of disused space above shops and offices in the town that could be adapted for this use.

Yours sincerely,

Theresa Green

Theresa Green and thirty-three others
Year 6 Earthy Primary School

A letter to the council, see page 79

Responses

Woodley Town Council

Dear Year 6,

The Chief Environmental Officer would like to thank you for your letter of May 1st. Your comments have been noted.

Yours sincerely,

Mr C. Menter
Administrative secretary.

with compliments

Woodley Town Council

Dear Ms Green,

Thank you for your letter regarding the proposed housing development on Cowmarsh allotments. I would like to say how refreshing it is to learn that at least some of our young people take local issues seriously enough to devote time to putting together such a clearly written and interesting letter as yours.

I am glad that you are beginning to appreciate the need for more housing in a thriving, modern and dynamic town such as ours. As you grow older, and begin to consider raising a family of your own, you will come to realize that not everyone would want to reside in converted space above a town centre shop. Most families like to have their own gardens, and in this respect the Cowmarsh site is ideal. Have you considered the idea that a garden can be just as rich in widlife habitats as an allotment?

Your concern for our senior citizens is commendable. We at the council share this concern, and will ensure that every effort is made to find alternative allotment plots for those who will be required to quit the Cowmarsh site. Your concern for those temporarily without work is also understandable, but I am sure that you will agree that the best remedy for persons in this position is to seek and find employment. The closure of the Cowmarsh site will give these people more time to do this, and the building jobs that will become available as a result of this development will no doubt provide opportunities for these people to begin to earn a living again.

Once again, thank you for your thoughtful letter.

Yours sincerely,

Councillor F.E. Seize

Scramble, see page 80

Story scrambles

AESTHETIC ICONOCLAST THROWS UP ANOTHER MUSHTERPIECE

This year's Turner prize for modern art has been won by one of London's most controversial contemporary artists, Professor Sheila Rastrick Farjeon. Professor Rastrick is a graduate of Goldmith's Art School, and was originally considered to be a misfit at that institution because of her preference for traditional media and subjects. Known to her arty chums as Far-Gone, this brainy young redhead has been packing the galleries with the sort of painting that makes the canvas look as if somebody has thrown up on it. After graduating in 1999, Professor Farjeon quickly abandoned her rebellious traditionalism, and began to explore the possibilities of representing unconventional landscapes using unconventional materials. One of the richest sources for her exploration of new media is the world of foodstuffs. Baked beans, treacle, strawberry jam, cock-a-leeky soup and squashed haggis – if the supermarket has it on the shelves, the wacky prof will smear it all over a canvas, spray it with quick setting varnish and give it a funny name. Then she'll stick a great big price tag on it, and nine times out of ten she'll get every penny she's asked for. The work with which Professor Farjeon won the Turner Prize is entitled 'Paving Stone: Plumstead High Street' and depicts the eponymous object in rich but ironically realistic spatters of tomato ketchup, grated chocolate and burnt custard. This uncompromising work has already been purchased for permanent exhibition in Woolwich Town Hall. So that's half a million pounds worth of council taxpayers' money straight into Far-Gone's bank account for an eyesore that could have been had a lot more cheaply by emptying a restaurant dustbin onto a big sheet of paper.

DIN-TINNABULATION WRECKS AUDITORY MEATUS, EAR-DOCS WARN

Top ear doctors are warning parents that they risk giving their kids GBH of the lugholes by buying them trendy personal stereos. Audiologist Peter Orpheus of The Great Harmond Street Hospital for Sick Children has disclosed that an increasing number of children referred with hearing problems have sustained irreversible damage to the delicate bone structure of the inner ear, probably caused by powerful vibrations directed into the ear by the mini-speakers of headsets. Alarm bells started ringing for the doctor when he heard one tot's headset blasting away from the far end of the corridor. "That child's skull had been absorbing more than twice the safe level of decibels, for several hours a day, since his birthday four months ago," the doctor said. "His eardrums were like colanders, and he'll be wearing a hearing aid until the day he dies." Audiologists in the USA and Europe have confirmed that a worrying rise in the level of childhood deafness has lead to concerns about the media effects of other fashion accessories such as mobile phones and singing ear-rings.

Newspapers now and then, see page 82

Old and new

Tea clipper 'Augustus' lost off Peddock's Island: Valiant Hull Life Preservation Team Avert Catastrophic Fatalities

Even in the midst of a winter characterized by furious demonstrations of elemental wrath, the furious tempest which ravaged the seas and nearby coastal communities of Massachusetts Bay in the hours before the cock-crow yesterday morning will live on in legend as one of the most momentous. Captain William Burke of the Augustus, three months from Trincomalee with a cargo of connoisseur tea and nutmeg, declared that in all of his days at sea, he had never witnessed the equal to the storm which wrecked his vessel and very nearly ended his life. The Augustus was a league off Peddock's making good headway for a dawn anchorage at Plymouth Rock when the first blasts of the gale ripped the shrouds from the rigging, meanwhile driving the ship headlong on to Shag Reef, splintering several timbers and bringing the main mast toppling down across the deck. Rockets were immediately launched, and amidst dark seas both mountainous and freezing, the valiant men of the Hull Life Preservation Team were roused from their slumbers. A full muster had assembled at the Gut within minutes, and Commander Joshua James, veteran of many a battle against the murderous waters that surround Hull Peninsula, supervised the launch of the lifeboat. 'Aye,' 'twas a challenging mission, and one in which prudence and expedition needed to be balanced in due measure,' Commander James said later.

Crew saved as teaship sinks

The remains of the tea clipper Augustus and her entire cargo are lying at the bottom of Massachusetts Bay this morning after the worst storm of a bad winter. Captain Bill Burke, speaking from his hospital bed just hours after a dramatic rescue by the Hull Lifesavers, said that it was the nastiest storm he had ever seen. 'We never stood a chance,' he said. 'After just one blast of this freak gale our sails were in ribbons and the ship was smashed wide open on Shag Reef. If it wasn't for Josh and the lads from Hull doing such a brilliant job we'd never have worn dry trousers again.'

Text comparison, see page 83

Hummingbirds

1 Hummingbirds are tiny creatures. The smallest variety, known as the bee hummingbird, weighs barely a gram and a half. In spite of their size, hummingbirds are perhaps the most vigorous of birds. They can beat their wings up to 200 times a second, movement so rapid that it renders the wings invisible and produces the noise that gives these birds their name. Hummingbirds can fly backwards as well as forwards, and can even fly upside down for brief periods. In order to fuel their high energy lives, hummingbirds eat up to half their weight in sugar each day, most of it taken from the nectar of flowers. They feed five to eight times an hour, using their long tongues to lap nectar at the rate of thirteen licks per second. Hummingbirds can also feed on tree sap, and on insects plucked from the air, foliage and spiders' webs.

2 Hummingbird hovered
Nectar turned to feathered light
Colour became life.

3 I used to go to school in Guyana. There was a garden full of huge, bright flowers surrounding the school, and rich perfumes would often drift through the wooden slats that served as windows. The garden was a favourite feeding place for hummingbirds. These tiny, shiny, colourful creatures beat their wings so rapidly as they darted from bloom to bloom that you could more often hear them than see them. They were like miniature angels, shimmering on the brink of invisibility as they flew, but when they hovered to sup from the flowers you could see their startling colours. One day I came into the classroom and found the body of a hummingbird on the floor. I assumed that it had flown in between the slats then beaten itself to death trying to get back out into the garden. I picked it up and sadly carried it outside, admiring its magnificent colours. Then I felt an electrical buzzing on my palm as the creature suddenly hummed into life and zoomed away, vanishing into the foliage. It had not been dead after all. It must have stunned itself in trying to escape, before reviving as soon as it felt the fresh air and the fragrance of the flowers.

4 The most important thing about hummingbirds is that they can beat their wings so rapidly that they become invisible. Hummingbirds live in warm countries. They have beautiful plumage. They are the smallest birds in the world. But the most important thing about hummingbirds is the rapidity of their wing movements.

The register, see page 84

Horoscope

 Aries: A good day is in store as long as you refuse to listen to flattery, and trust to your own sound judgements. The Sun's link with Neptune should ensure that people pay attention to your creative ideas.

 Taurus: Anybody who has ever doubted your determination to get things done and done well is about to be proved wrong. The influence of the Bull is at its peak today, and you can't really go wrong.

 Gemini: Today will be the worst day of your life. If by some miracle you manage to survive all the horrors and catastrophes that your nasty little ruler Mercury will bring down on you, you will end this day wishing that you had never been born.

 Cancer: What a superb day for reflecting on the riches of the past and looking forward to the promises of the future! A happy alignment between Neptune and the Moon will ensure that today is rich with good feelings.

 Leo: Today will be as good, bad or indifferent as any other day. It is impossible to predict from the stars anything about what life has on offer for you today, or on any other day for that matter. You'll just have to see how it goes.

 Virgo: Perhaps it's time for you to face that difficult decision or awkward little job that you have been avoiding? Venus is in the ascendant, so there is no better time for you to grasp the nettle and put your best foot forward. You'll feel better for it afterwards!

 Libra: Lucky old you! The circumstances are just right today for you to throw caution to the winds and take that gamble you've been considering for the last week. You might not achieve all that you've hoped for, but the risk will be worth it.

 Scorpio: If you want to make significant changes to your love life or career, now is the time to swing into action. Take a good long look at your current situation and decide what you want to keep and what you could do without. A stitch in time saves nine!

 Sagittarius: Speak up now if you want to be heard. Your old friend the Archer won't let you down and will ensure that a friendly ear is turned to your opinions. You have something to say, so say it!

 Capricorn: You will lose your bag on the way to work or school today. It will be handed in to the police station tomorrow, but this will be too late for you to avoid missing that ten o'clock appointment on which your future depends. Tough luck!

 Aquarius: Grab every chance you can to do good to your friends and colleagues today. Your naturally sunny nature will be further polished by the ascent of Uranus, and you will end the day glowing.

 Pisces: Can you really afford to relax quite so much as you've been tempted to recently? At least 50 per cent of your former friends now regard you as a lazy parasite, and with your sign star dipping towards the equinox it is very likely that today your sins will find you out!

The register, see page 84

Advertisements

▶ **Does your house stink?**

YES ✔ NO ☐

▶ **Is your kitchen full of flies and cockroaches?**

YES ✔ NO ☐

▶ **Are you too bone idle to clean the place up?**

YES ✔ NO ☐

THEN YOU NEED

The all purpose room freshener and insecticide. Slobmate has been specially formulated to fill smelly houses like yours with the reek of fake roses.

It is guaranteed to exterminate all non-human household vermin without you needing to lift a finger, so you can go on living in squalor without the annoyance of the neighbours complaining about odours and pests.

Why is Slobmate so effective?

Because it contains some of the most powerful life-destroying chemicals known to man!

But rest assured – there is no risk to you!

So buy Slobmate – the product that lets you live the life you choose!

Most dental authorities

now agree that using toothpaste is a waste of time and money, and that you can look after your teeth just as well by brushing them with tap water. Just in case they are wrong, we have introduced a new brand of toothpaste which we call

TOOTHPASTE

It is white and creamy and comes in a tube. You squeeze some out onto a brush and clean your teeth with it, then you spit it out and swill your mouth with water.

It has artificial mint flavouring in it, and it is not poisonous. It costs about a pound a tube. If you buy it it might do you some good, and it will help us to stay in business.

Wordplay compendium, see page 88

Playing with words

Secret languages

Eeny meeny macka racka rara raya dominacka chicka pocka lollipopa im pom push aye!

Michelle fifichelle chickelichelle bombichelle bombichelle fifichelle-
That's how you spell Michelle!

My mavourite feal is pashed motatoes with bausages and saked seans in somato tause.

Jack-sack-lack and-sand-land Jill-sill-lill went-sent-lent up-sup-lup the-se-le hill-sill-lill.

ethay atcay atsay onway ethy atmay.

Alphabet sentences

Quick love, fix me up with a dozen brandy jugs.

King Henry ate fishy squid jam with six very oozy black peas.

Palindromes

Draw pupil's lip upward.
Marge let Sharon eye Norah's telegram.
I roamed under it as a tired nude Maori.
Straw? No, too stupid a fad. I put soot on warts.

Four letter stories

When Mark told Jean that Leo's rats were more like cats than mice,
Alan said, "don't make such dumb gags, chum."
Then Mark fell over onto Leo's cage. Leo's four poor rats died flat.
Eyes wide, lips open, Jean went grey.
"Take that, punk!"
Alan, wild with rage, shot Mark.
Mark said, "Alan, your fury just isn't what folk need."
Then, face cold, Mark died.
Alan wept.
Jean, more hard than Alan, said, "this girl don't fear dead lads, mate.
Pray don't shed such loud, long sobs. Into each life some rain must fall."

Alphabet stories

A bold caveman drew eight fleeing gazelles high inside, joyfully kicking light mud. Now, or perhaps quite recently, scientists tested uglier views with x-rays, yearning zestfully.

Creating clear instructions, see page 89

Apple crumble

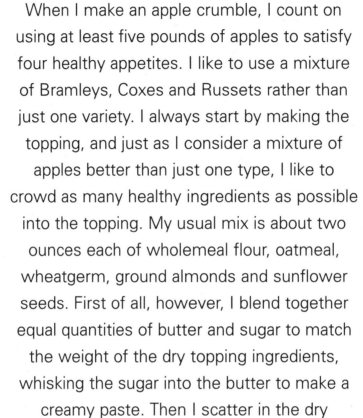

When I make an apple crumble, I count on using at least five pounds of apples to satisfy four healthy appetites. I like to use a mixture of Bramleys, Coxes and Russets rather than just one variety. I always start by making the topping, and just as I consider a mixture of apples better than just one type, I like to crowd as many healthy ingredients as possible into the topping. My usual mix is about two ounces each of wholemeal flour, oatmeal, wheatgerm, ground almonds and sunflower seeds. First of all, however, I blend together equal quantities of butter and sugar to match the weight of the dry topping ingredients, whisking the sugar into the butter to make a creamy paste. Then I scatter in the dry ingredients bit by bit until the mixture resembles breadcrumbs. When this has been done, I slice the apples and lay them in layers in a big casserole dish, squeezing a segment of lemon over each layer to stop them from going brown. Finally, I cover the apples with the topping, dot the surface with an extra ounce of butter, and bake the lot in a moderate oven until the topping is crisp and the apples are bubbling up through the crust.